What is
Gender History?

What is History?

John H. Arnold, *What is Medieval History?*

Peter Burke, *What is Cultural History?*

John C. Burnham, *What is Medical History?*

Pamela Kyle Crossley, *What is Global History?*

Christiane Harzig and Dirk Hoerder, *What is Migration History?*

Andrew Hinde, *What is Population History?*

J. Donald Hughes, *What is Environmental History?*

Andrew Leach, *What is Architectural History?*

Stephen Morillo and Michael Pavkovic, *What is Military History?*

Sonya O. Rose, *What is Gender History?*

What is
Gender History?

SONYA O. ROSE

polity

First published in 2010 by Polity Press

Polity Press
65 Bridge Street
Cambridge CB2 1UR, UK

Polity Press
350 Main Street
Malden, MA 02148, USA

ISBN-13: 978-0-7456-4614-5
ISBN-13: 978-0-7456-4615-2(pb)

A catalogue record for this book is available from the British Library.

Typeset in 10.5 on 12 pt Sabon
by Toppan Best-set Premedia Limited
Printed and bound in Great Britain by MPG Books Group Limited, Bodmin, Cornwall

The publisher has used its best endeavours to ensure that the URLs for external websites referred to in this book are correct and active at the time of going to press. However, the publisher has no responsibility for the websites and can make no guarantee that a site will remain live or that the content is or will remain appropriate.

Every effort has been made to trace all copyright holders, but if any have been inadvertently overlooked the publisher will be pleased to include any necessary credits in any subsequent reprint or edition.

For further information on Polity, visit our website:
www.politybooks.com

#6010088703

Contents

Preface and Acknowledgements   vi

1   Why Gender History?   1

2   Bodies and Sexuality in Gender History   17

3   Gender and Other Relations of Difference   36

4   Men and Masculinity   56

5   Gender and Historical Knowledge   80

6   Assessing "Turns" and New Directions   102

Notes   122

Suggestions for Further Reading   138

Index   147

Preface and Acknowledgements

This book is primarily about what gender historians do. It is not a history of gender, but rather it is about approaches to the field and their development, and considers some of the topics in history that have concerned gender historians. I have tried throughout to focus on gender or the meanings and expectations concerning what it means to be male or female. It is not a book about women's history, although there is some discussion of the field and its contributions to gender history. The primary purpose of this volume is to provide an introduction to the subject both for students who have had some training in history but have not previously encountered gender history as a field, and for students who have studied women and gender in other disciplines but have not had the opportunity to learn about how historians approach these topics. The book takes up certain controversies that have developed among scholars of women's and gender history, it provides an overview of some of the complexities in studying gender history, and it considers new directions in the field. This should make it useful to more advanced students and scholars who might find such an overview of value.

Chapter 1 provides basic definitions of the terms "gender," "history," and "feminist history." It charts the development of gender history from women's history and discusses its uneven influence on scholarship. Chapter 2 complicates the distinction between sex and gender and considers histories of the body and histories of sexuality. Chapter 3 takes up gender and its intersections with race and class using as examples among other topics, slavery, and colonialism. Chapter 4 introduces the reader to the study of men and masculinity, discussing different approaches to the topic and emphasizing the changing understandings of masculinity over time as well as the various ways that manhood is understood and practiced in a given historical period. Chapter 5 illustrates how historians of gender have contributed to questions that have been central to historians generally. It focuses especially on colonial conquest, revolution, nationalism, and war and covers examples from the seventeenth to the twentieth centuries. Chapter 6 examines some of the controversies over approaches to studying gender in history, and introduces the reader to some of the new directions being taken, including psychoanalytic and other approaches to subjectivity, and transnational or global histories. It serves, as well, as a review or reminder of some of the other issues and topics covered in the book.

The book is written as an engaged overview that attempts both to synthesize how scholars have approached the field and to give fairly detailed examples of historical scholarship on particular topics of concern to gender historians. It is impossible for such a book to cover everything in a domain of inquiry as diverse and rich as gender history, and thus I have attempted to provide the reader with a sense of the kinds of questions gender historians ask and how they have gone about answering them. While the text draws heavily from work on North America and Britain, I have also attempted to provide examples from across the world. As my own work specializes in modern history, especially the nineteenth and twentieth centuries, this is the focus of much of the book. However, I have also included some discussion of the exciting work done by scholars whose work is on periods ranging from the thirteenth through the eighteenth centuries. I wanted to give some idea of the histories of particular topics from a variety of regions and/or countries and time periods, and although such examples might seem to lack historical context – because their histories will simply be less familiar – it is my hope that the reader will nonetheless be able to learn from them some of what these gender historians have discovered in their research.

I am indebted to a host of feminist historians whose work has inspired me over the years. I cannot hope to list them all here, nor will they necessarily find their work specifically cited in the text. Many of them, however, will be included in the topically organized list of selected readings at the end of the book. Thanks also are especially due to Andrea Drugan at Polity, who has been a model of what an editor should be – supportive, encouraging, and quick to respond to various drafts and queries, and to Justin Dyer, for a heroic and truly helpful job of copy-editing. I would also like to thank the anonymous reviewers for Polity and my London friends, Catherine Hall, Keith McClelland, and Bill Schwarz, for listening to my concerns as I worked on this book. Special thanks go to Sue Juster for suggesting examples of particularly interesting scholarship on gender in Colonial North America. Most especially, I thank Guenter Rose for his patience and support and for putting up with the angst I experienced as I found writing this book to be a much more difficult and complex undertaking than I had anticipated.

1
Why Gender History?

In answering the question posed by the title of this book, "what is gender history?" I hope to convince the reader that gender both has a history and is historically significant. To begin, we must first consider what might seem self-evident but is, in fact, complex – how to think about history itself.

History is comprised of knowledge about the past. This means that history is the product of scholarship concerning the past. At this point the reader might wonder, isn't history *the past*? Common sense would tell us that if someone is interested in history, that person is interested in what has happened before the present day. But it is important to be clear that the past is *reconstructed* through historical scholarship – the knowledge produced by historians. This suggests that the process of reconstruction is all-important in the knowledge that is produced. What we know about the past is dependent upon the questions historians have asked and how they have answered them. What has been the focus of their interest? What have they deemed to be important to study about the past? How have they gone about studying it? How have they interpreted the evidence they have unearthed? To complicate matters, the answers to these questions themselves have changed over time. Historians are not outside of history, but are shaped by it and by the political, cultural, social, and economic climates in which they live and work. Thus, history itself has a history. This is important background to keep in mind as we begin to explore the topics of gender and gender history.

Although historians have differed and continue to differ in their approaches to their subject, they would all share the following assumption: the conditions within which people live their lives and the societies which shape those conditions change over time. These changes are many and varied, and the rates at which transformations occur also are variable. But the presumption of change or transformation is fundamental to historical scholarship. Not all historical scholarship, however, charts and accounts for changes. While some historians are concerned to show how events and certain processes were instrumental in transforming a society or an aspect of society, others are interested in exploring the processes producing continuities over time, and still others are involved in projects that describe aspects of life in a particular period or set of years in the past. But although such historians may not focus on change *per se*, they assume that the characteristics of the lives they unearth and write about are products of social and cultural processes that take place through time.

Gender history is based on the fundamental idea that what it means to be defined as man or woman has a history. Gender historians are concerned with the changes over time and the variations within a single society in a particular period in the past with regard to the perceived differences between women and men, the make-up of their relationships, and the nature of the relations among women and among men as gendered beings. They are concerned with *how* these differences and relationships are historically produced and how they are transformed. Importantly, they are also concerned with the impact of gender on a variety of historically important events and processes. In order to more fully explore the concerns of gender historians and how they "do" gender history, it is crucial to consider the meaning of the term "gender."

Scholars use the concept of gender to denote the perceived differences between and ideas about women and men, male and female. Fundamental to the definition of the term "gender" is the idea that these differences are socially constructed. What it means to be man and what it means to be woman, the definitions or understandings of masculinity and femininity, the characteristics of male and female identities – all are the products of culture. Why use the term "gender" rather than the term "sex"? Why speak of the differences between men and women, or males and females, as gender differences rather than sex differences? In very recent years and as the next chapter will discuss in more detail, sex and gender have been considered synonyms and frequently are used interchangeably in popular discourse. But the term "gender" was originally used by feminist scholars to mean the cultural construction of sex difference, in contrast to the term "sex," which was thought to mean "natural" or "biological" difference.

Before the last decades of the twentieth century and the growth and impact of scholarship on women and gender in numerous disciplines, including anthropology, history, and sociology, it was popularly assumed that the differences between men and women were based in nature and that these "natural differences" accounted for or explained the observed differences in women's and men's social positions and social relationships, their ways of being in the world, and the differences between them in various forms of power. Importantly, the hierarchical nature of the relations between men and women was assumed and not questioned. The presumption that the various differences between women and men were based in nature rather than being products of culture meant that it took particular historical circumstances to occur for scholars to begin to think that gender had a history or histories and that gender mattered to history.

Gender history developed in response to the scholarship on and debates about women's history. As a field of study, women's history began to flower only in the late 1960s and flourished in the 1970s, continuing to this day as a crucial component of gender history. But even before this, histories of women had been written, so that the development of the field from the 1960s may be considered a revival or renaissance, but in a new context that encouraged its formation as an academic field of study. Histories of women written before the twentieth century generally concerned such figures as queens and saints. For the most part the lives of ordinary women went unrecorded and unremarked upon except for the work of a few important predecessors to contemporary women's history who wrote during the first half of the twentieth century. These important predecessors included Eileen Power, Alice Clark, and Ivy Pinchbeck in Britain and Julia Spruill and Mary Beard in the United States. Disregarding their work, professional historians considered the activities of women as mothers and wives, servants, workers, and consumers irrelevant to history. The histories of women written before the late 1960s and 1970s were generally not integrated into professional or popular histories of the time.

Why was it that women had been ignored by "mainstream historians"? A primary reason, one recognized early on in the development of the new women's history, was that women had been neglected as historical subjects because historians viewed history to be almost singularly about the exercise and transmission of power in the realms of politics and economics, arenas in which the actors were men. The rise of women's history and its development contributed to a rethinking of historical practice that was taking place among social historians who considered knowledge about the everyday lives of ordinary people as important to making sense of the past. But social historians, too, ignored women as historical actors because they mistakenly understood men, especially white, European, and North American men, as the universal agents of history. For example, "workers" were imagined as male figures, and so labor history neglected women's work in the fields, workshops, and factories as well as in their homes.

Historians of women began to discover that women as well as men had been labor and community activists, social reformers, and political revolutionaries, and they demonstrated how women's labor contributed to their households and to the economy more broadly. Importantly, women's historians eventually challenged what had been a narrow definition of politics and power, broadening their scope to include arenas of life outside of governments and political parties, particularly in people's "private lives." These scholars delved into topics that had previously been considered "natural" rather than cultural or social, such as family violence, prostitution, and childbirth. These challenges to traditional historical practice came out of the very historical developments contributing to the rise and progress of women's history.

Women's history as a field of inquiry was a product of the women's movement, or what has been called "second-wave feminism," distinguishing it from the feminist movement of the nineteenth and early twentieth centuries, which sought to gain the vote for women as well as raising a number of other issues relating to women's inequality. Feminism was central in stimulating interest in and generating analytical approaches to the history of women. While those who consider themselves to be feminists today may not be in total agreement about precisely what the project of feminism should be, most would agree that fundamental to feminism is the belief that women should have the same basic human rights as men. Feminists argue that generally women are disadvantaged relative to men. They suffer such disadvantages because of how gender has patterned their social worlds. The idea that women everywhere should have the same advantages as men led feminist scholars to want to recover the previously untold story of women's lives in the past, to uncover the reasons for women's subordinate status, and to wonder about the apparent omission or exclusion of women from the historical record. As two US-based European historians, Renate Bridenthal and Claudia Koonz, wrote in the introduction to their aptly entitled collection, *Becoming Visible: Women in European History*, published in 1977, "The essays written for this volume seek both to restore women to history and to explore the meaning of women's unique historical experience."[1]

While the women's movement generally stimulated interest in women's history, the paths taken by feminist scholars varied depending upon the national context in which they worked. The place of women in the profession of history internationally differed with their institutional cultures – some were more open to women scholars than others. Women's history developed relatively quickly in the United States, for example, as women scholars began gaining institutional support in some universities early in the 1970s. In Britain, institutional support developed later, and feminist-inspired historians there began to do women's history from outside of the academy. But into the late 1980s women's history still lacked academic respectability, and even today feminist historians are struggling to have women and gender incorporated into some areas of historical writing. In France and Germany, women's history has been even slower to gain the acceptance of professional male historians.

Although women's historians all were motivated by feminism, the substance and direction of women's history as a field developed somewhat differently in different national settings.[2] In the United States, the concept of "separate spheres" became highly influential. In search of the roots of women's subjugation and to recover the texture of and influences on women's lives in the past, scholars depicted them as living and acting in a distinct space and or realm of activities centered on their families and households. As Linda Kerber has noted, historians discovered the use of the term "women's sphere" in their sources, and that discovery, in turn, "directed the choices made by twentieth-century historians about what to study and how to tell the stories that they reconstructed."[3] In an enormously influential 1966 essay about American women's lives in the years 1820–60, Barbara Welter described what she called the "Cult of True Womanhood," an ideology prescribing that women should live by and for the virtues of "piety, purity, submissiveness, and domesticity."[4] Welter focused her inquiry on white, Northern, middle-class women, using as sources such written material as advice books, sermons, and women's magazines. Although as the field of women's history changed and diversified it was to be criticized by scholars for being based only on prescriptive literature and for its attention to only one group of women, Welter's analysis kick-started what was to be a dominant emphasis in the US field generally into the 1980s. While being descriptive, it also was critical of the patriarchal relations that confined women and defined their lives, and like other works of the women's history revival, it emphasized women's oppression. Importantly, Welter suggested that the cult inspired diverse responses, and coupled with larger societal changes, including the abolitionist movement and the Civil War, women expanded their activities beyond the narrowly domestic realm.

"Women's sphere" in nineteenth-century US history was analyzed by some feminist scholars in the mid-1970s and into the early 1980s as the source of what became described as a "women's culture." Scholars developing the idea of "women's culture" were not focused primarily on analyzing how and why women were victims of a patriarchal society. Rather, they were interested in exploring the centrality of the relationships among women in history. In an important essay, Carroll Smith-Rosenberg, for example, argued on the basis of her analysis of numerous letters and diaries that in order to understand women's lives in nineteenth-century America, it was crucial to examine their relationships with one another. Women, she argued, as relatives, neighbors, and friends, spent their everyday lives together. Women's friendships were characterized by devotion and solidarity, and were emotionally central in their lives. She further suggested that some Victorian women's relationships involved physical sensuality and possibly sexuality as well as emotional affection from adolescence into adulthood. For Smith-Rosenberg, women's sphere was not just a separate one, it had "an essential integrity and dignity that grew out of women's shared experiences and mutual affection."[5] Nancy Cott moved the idea of "women's sphere" onto new ground in her analysis of the development of the ideology of domesticity and women's sphere from 1780 to 1835. The title of her book, *The Bonds of Womanhood*, was meant to underscore the double meaning of the term "bonds" as both constraints and connections.[6] Using diaries in addition to prescriptive literature, she revealed some of the oppressive consequences of the ideology of domesticity, but more importantly she showed that a sense of sisterhood was nurtured within women's sphere, as a consequence of which some women became politically conscious as women and organized to promote their rights.

In Britain, feminist historical research was stimulated by both the women's movement and socialist or Marxian-inspired social and labor history. In the 1970s and early 1980s, feminist historians were keen to understand how women's lives and activities were simultaneously affected by sex-based and class-based divisions. Sheila Rowbotham's significant publications in the 1970s were influenced both by Marxism and by feminism. In her 1973 *Women's Consciousness, Man's World*, she argued for the necessity of understanding the "precise relationship between the patriarchal dominance of men over women, and the property relations which come from this, to class exploitation and racism."[7] In *Hidden from History* published in the same year she surveyed the impact of capitalism on the lives of women in the late eighteenth and early nineteenth centuries and critically explored women's participation in both feminist and socialist projects.[8] Sally Alexander's mid-1970s feminist-inspired research critically addressed Marx's ideas about the capitalist mode of production.[9] She argued that the sexual division of labor, articulated by and reproduced within the family when the household was the unit of production, continued to shape industrial capitalism as industrial methods were transformed in nineteenth-century London. Alexander maintained that this dynamic involving the impact of the household division of labor on industrial transformation should be central to feminist historical research.

A significant study by Jill Liddington and Jill Norris of northern British working-class women's participation in the struggle for the vote, published in 1978, carefully explored the connections between their suffrage activism, their work and family lives, and their involvement in trade unionism.[10] Based on interviews with the daughters of these suffragists as well as a wealth of archival sources, Liddington and Norris' study reconstructed the suffrage activities in which these women engaged, often in the face of the hostility from the men in their lives, and their cooperation with one another in carrying out their domestic duties so that they could continue their political work.

Making use of the social and economic historians' concept of "family economy," Laura Oren showed that the sexual divisions within the household caused women's diets as well as their children's to suffer relative to men.[11] Women stretched household expenses that husbands allotted to them from their pay to assure that their husbands were well taken care of, while men kept pocket money for themselves to use for their own necessities as well as pleasures. Oren concluded that the wife's management of the household budget served as a buffer both for her husband in hard times, and for the economy and industrial system more generally.

Although the study of working-class women was a predominant focus of women's historians in Britain, the ideology of separate spheres and the split between the primarily middle-class private, domestic world of women and the family and men's public worlds concerned some women's historians there as well as in the United States. Leonore Davidoff and her colleagues, for example, focused on what they called the "beau idyll," the image of peaceful, bourgeois family life in suburban towns that were developed to imitate life in rural villages. At its center was the separation of women and the family from the concerns of the public arena, giving women "their own sphere of influence in the home."[12] The domestic/public division was not, in their view, a timeless feature of social life, but rather it was an historically emerging ideology connected to the development of the competitive economic world of business. This ideology was instrumental in creating the domestic ideals and spaces of middle-class women's lived lives.

While some British feminist historians were concerned with domestic ideology and its consequences for middle-class women, a growing number of US feminist scholars turned to women's labor and working-class history. In the mid-1970s, Alice Kessler-Harris asked, "Where are the organized women workers?" and her research on early twentieth-century US workers pointed to the decided ambivalence of male unionists to working women, the low level of support that major US trade union organizations gave to women organizers, and employers' efforts to prevent women from organizing.[13] In the early 1980s Kessler-Harris published a history of US wage-earning women from the colonial period to post-World War II.[14] The book highlights the various ways in which women's economic opportunities were limited and the changes in the relationship between family and work from the nineteenth century to the last half of the twentieth century.

Other important works on women's labor and working-class history in the United States include Thomas Dublin's research on women working in the Lowell, Massachusetts textile industry between the 1820s and 1860, Jacqueline Jones' landmark study of black working women from slavery to the post-World War II period, and Christine Stansell's study of working-class women in New York City between 1780 and 1860. Dublin's research, based on extensive company archival records, memoirs, and letters, detailed the growth of the textile industry and the recruitment of young women from rural New England to work in the mills.[15] He examined the community these women established in Lowell, the protests they organized over low wages and poor working conditions, and the subsequent transformation of the industry and decline of women's labor activism as the workforce diversified. Jacqueline Jones' study of black women workers investigates the sexual division of labor in the fields under slavery, and after the Civil War, the high value accorded black working women in their own communities, and how race discrimination forced them into the lowest paid and most menial forms of labor.[16] She shows their commitment to the economic welfare of their families despite the degraded nature of their work. Christine Stansell's research explored the nature of the communities that young workers created in early nineteenth-century New York City and she investigated the changing nature of women's place in the family economy, their increasing opportunities to earn wages with the expansion of "outwork" in manufacturing allowing them to earn money working at home, and the neighborhood networks that they formed for mutual support.[17]

Radical feminism was another path taken by women's historians in both Britain and the United States. Radical feminists viewed women's oppression as a consequence of patriarchal dominance and thus saw the problem of men's power over women (or patriarchy) as the central problem to be analyzed by women's historians. As the London Feminist History Group put it, "[W]omen have not just been hidden from history. They have been deliberately oppressed. Recognition of this oppression is one of the central tenets of feminism."[18] This did not mean that women should be viewed only as victims. Rather, women's historians working within this general framework were concerned to show the ways that women resisted their oppression. Thus, for example, in their discussion of separate spheres, the London Feminist History Group suggested that it was important for histories to be written showing that women's activities that ranged beyond the domestic realm into the world of politics and the professions were "directly resisting men's dominance and control of these areas," even as they faced considerable opposition from men who controlled their movement.[19]

Important studies focusing on women in the past from the various feminist perspectives continued to be produced into the 1980s. Increasingly, however, critical voices were heard. Some were concerned that there was a tendency in women's history to assume a universal women's experience, ignoring differences among women not only of class, but of race, sexual preference, and ethnic, national, or religious backgrounds. Increasingly, feminist scholars became concerned that the research intended to recover women's lives in the past to bring them into the historical record, regardless of the theoretical position informing it, produced a history of women that was isolated from the history of men, reinforcing the "ghettoization" or marginalization of feminist history.

In the mid-1970s two US-based European women's historians suggested an approach to feminist history that a decade later was to be elaborated into what we now know as "gender history." Joan Kelly-Gadol, arguing that "compensatory" women's history would not transform how history is written, suggested that the "social relation of the sexes" ought to be at the center of feminist history.[20] At about the same time, Natalie Zemon Davis proposed that to correct the bias in the historical record, it would be necessary to look at both women and men – "the significance of the sexes of gender groups in the past." This, she suggested "should help promote a rethinking of some of the central issues faced by historians – power, social structure, property, symbols and periodization."[21]

Although socialist feminist scholars in Britain were intent upon broadening Marxist theory to include a focus on women and sex difference, it was in the United States that the term "gender" first became central to understanding women's lives in the past. Scholars there began to question the concept of women's culture or the existence of a separate female world and attempted to take into account questions of race, class, and ethnicity. For example, in their introduction to a book of essays, *Sex and Class in Women's History*, the editors, US-based historians of America and Britain, Judith Newton, Mary Ryan, and Judith Walkowitz, stated explicitly that in thinking about women's history, they would "employ gender as a category of historical analysis."[22] Their purpose in using the category was "to understand the systematic ways in which sex differences have cut through society and culture and in the process have conferred inequality upon women."[23]

The shift to a focus on gender through the late 1970s and into the mid-1980s also is apparent in the Introduction to the second edition of *Becoming Visible: Women in European History*, published in 1987. The editors of the new edition, Renate Bridenthal, Claudia Koonz, and Susan Stuard, comment that they intend not only to make women visible, but also to "examine the socially constructed and historically changing gender systems that divide masculine from feminine roles."[24]

While the concept of "gender" was becoming increasingly influential in the early and mid-1980s, it was Joan Scott's theoretical intervention, published in the December 1985 issue of *American Historical Review*, that was to have a major impact on the development of gender history as a field of scholarship. To answer questions such as how gender works in social relationships and how it influences historical knowledge, it is necessary, she argued, to conceptualize gender in a theoretically rigorous manner.[25] She maintained that such a theoretical approach, rather than one that describes women's lives in the past, is necessary if feminist scholarship is to transform historical studies. While, as we have seen, feminist scholars earlier had been using the term "gender" and had argued for its significance, Scott offered a new approach that did not focus on the recovery of women's activities in the past, but instead queried how gender worked to distinguish masculine from feminine. She defined gender as the meanings given to the perceived differences between the sexes. The primary questions for Scott concerned how "the subjective and collective meanings of women and men as categories of identity have been constructed."[26] Influenced by French post-structuralism, Scott insisted that meaning is constructed and communicated through language or discourse which inevitably involves differentiations or contrasts. These differentiations or oppositions, including the dichotomy of male and female, are both interdependent (male is only meaningful in contrast to female) and they are inherently unstable (because of the intrinsic heterogeneity of all categories). All dichotomies, including the dichotomy of male and female, vary over time and across societies. But such binary oppositions appear to be timeless because the politics involved in establishing them have been obscured. It is the historian's job to recover them for the historical record.

One of the most important aspects of Scott's theory of gender is her proposition that gender is a primary way of signifying relationships of power – gender is a critical means by which power is expressed or legitimated. Mrinalini Sinha has shown, for example, how the stereotypes of the "manly Englishman" and the "effeminate Bengali" served to legitimate colonial rule and racial hierarchy in late nineteenth-century India, and both emerged from and shaped various political controversies in India and Britain.[27]

Scott's ideas had an enormous impact on numerous feminist historians as they contributed to and participated in what became known in academic history circles as the cultural or linguistic "turn." Increasingly the terms "discourse" and "text" and a focus on the production of meanings appeared in scholarship. But Scott's theoretical approach and the turn to gender more generally was and continues to be controversial.

While Scott's advocacy of French post-structuralism was drawn upon by numerous feminist historians to analyze the language of gender in various historical contexts, this theoretical position met with criticism and considerable hostility from others. Scott's primary concern with language and representation and with unstable meanings enraged some feminist scholars for denying "retrievable historical 'reality.'"[28] As Joan Hoff put it, in this approach "material experiences become abstract representations drawn almost exclusively from textual analysis; personal identities and all human agency become obsolete, and disembodied subjects are constructed by discourses. Flesh-and-blood women...also become social constructs."[29] In stressing the primacy of language, Scott questioned the concept of "experience," suggesting that experience is unknowable outside of language and thus it is itself discursively produced. But there were feminist historians who feared that without a concept of experience outside of its textual production there was nothing that women shared on which to ground a feminist politics. The idea that "woman" was only a social construction seemed to some scholars to deny the existence of women and thus to deny them "a position from which they can speak, based on their embodied experience of womanhood."[30]

Critics of the turn to gender as well as post-structuralism were concerned that by opening gender history to the study of men, women would again be obscured from the historical record. Furthermore, some argued that the result of focusing on the symbolic link between gender and power could well sidestep historical questions about the operation of "patriarchy," the inequalities in power between women as a group compared to men.[31] While concern about the relationship between women's history and gender history persists among some feminist historians, others applaud the contributions of gender history and defend it against some of the criticisms that have been leveled at it. As to the charge that a focus on differences among women and on the instability of the meaning of the category "woman" as a social construction diminishes a common ground on which women can create a feminist politics, it has been argued that only by recognizing diversity and difference and acknowledging the multiple and possibly conflicting ways in which identities are formed is it possible to create political ties among women. Gender history's attention to men and masculinity emphasizes the idea that masculinity and femininity exist in relation to one another. Focusing on men as gendered beings corrects the assumption that masculinity is some sort of unchanging "natural" state of being and that men's historical agency can be understood without taking gender and sexuality into account. Acknowledging the diversity among men and working with the idea that there are multiple masculinities forged in relation to one another as well as in relation to women does not deny that generally men are more powerful than women. Indeed, as US historians Nancy Cott and Drew Gilpin Faust have maintained, it is because gender has been understood as a hierarchical formation, not simply one of difference but one of domination, that gender has been a way of signifying relations of power.[32]

There can be no doubt but that Joan Scott's intervention stimulated the development of gender history especially in North America and Britain, even if many practitioners did not follow her post-structuralist approach but used other, more traditional methods of analysis. In 1989 the journal,

Gender & History was founded in Britain by Leonore Davidoff with two editorial boards, one in the United Kingdom and one in the United States. In its inaugural issue the editors indicated their intention to take a feminist perspective that would address men and masculinity as well as women and femininity, "traditionally male institutions as well as those defined commonly as female"; and they indicated their encouragement of multiple approaches by recognizing that gender is "not only a set of lived relations; it is also a symbolic system."[33]

Although its founding editorial collectives were in Britain and North America, and it was an English-language journal, the editors not only welcomed an interdisciplinary perspective, but encouraged contributions from scholars of other nationalities and languages. Yet, the impact of Scott's initial challenge and the turn to gender history more generally was to be more profound in the Anglophone world than elsewhere. This does not mean that gender histories were written only about North America and Britain and Ireland, but that gender histories of Asia, Latin America, Eastern Europe, and so on, were more likely to be produced by scholars working in English-speaking countries (including Australia and New Zealand). There were a number of reasons for this. First, feminist history generally had a slower impact on the historical professions in countries where the historical profession was less open to women's history as well as to non-traditional approaches to historical analysis. Second, the term "gender" itself does not necessarily have equivalents in other languages. Also, cultural differences may have been at play. In France, for example, the closest equivalent to the term "gender" is *genre*, which refers both to grammatical gender and to literary genre. With some notable exceptions, French scholars were reluctant to adopt "imported concepts," and they rejected a hierarchical understanding of male–female relationships in favor of a complementary view of those relationships.[34] In China there is a fairly long tradition of historical scholarship on women produced by male scholars. This tradition of scholarship is based on the view that the distinction between man and woman (in Chinese, *nan/nu*) is a basic organizing principle of society. Yet, the concept of "gender" as it has been used in the Anglophone world has been slow to gain acceptance by Chinese academics, perhaps due to an assumption by Chinese historians of women that the relationship between men and women is a "harmonious" one. Historians and other scholars there, for example, have been slow to recognize men and masculinity as gendered beings.[35]

Conclusion

This chapter has introduced the reader to some of the basic conceptual issues in the study of gender and history, including defining both history and gender. It has traced the origins of gender history through the development of women's history in North America and Britain and discussed questions about history that arose as a consequence. The chapter has suggested that the turn to "gender" was stimulated by the concerns of some historians that women's history was merely "added" on to the historical record, but that it had not changed how basic historical issues were understood by professional historians. Gender history also was spurred by theoretical advances, especially French post-structuralism, whose influence on historical practice was greatly enhanced through the uses of it made by feminist historians. The advancement of gender history has led feminist scholars to ask new questions about gender as a category of analysis. Can gender have variable meanings across time and space? Have all societies in all time periods distinguished male and female on the basis of perceived bodily differences? And is there some fixed distinction between sex and gender? The next chapter will turn to some of these questions.

2
Bodies and Sexuality in Gender History

The distinction between sex and gender had been useful for feminist scholars as they investigated the histories of the perceived differences between women and men and explored the historical effects of those differences. But even as more and more scholars adopted gender as a "useful category of historical analysis," feminist cultural critics, philosophers, and historians of science became increasingly uncomfortable with the sex/gender distinction. At the very end of the twentieth century, historian Joan Scott, whose essay on gender as a useful category of historical analysis was a critical stimulus to the field of gender history in the mid-1980s, questioned whether the distinction between sex and gender made sense, arguing that a primary question to be asked concerns how "sexual difference" is articulated "as a principle and practice of social organization."[1] Moreover, in 2006, Mary Ryan chose the title *The Mysteries of Sex* for her book examining how the meanings of male and female have changed and varied through American history.[2]

Feminist scholars have noted several problems with the sex/gender distinction. One such problem is that sex and gender are frequently used interchangeably in popular discourse, with gender being deployed as a polite synonym for sex. One might read in the daily press, for example, that both genders were present at a political rally. If the two terms are synonymous, why keep the terminological distinction? Often, too, gender has been interpreted as meaning "women," as if "men" were not gendered beings. But other, more serious problems with the sex/gender distinction underpin this sort of confusion. If gender is a cultural interpretation of sex understood as biological or natural or as referring to physical, material bodies, then gender ultimately is based upon bodily difference, which is considered outside of or untouched by history or culture.

It may seem to be common sense that sex difference is in the realm of nature rather than culture. And that is precisely the problem. We commonly understand what is "natural" or "biological" to be unchangeable or fixed. If gender is supposed to be a cultural interpretation of sex, understood as "natural," there must be limits to how gender can shape understandings of sexual difference. The concept of sexual difference, then, retains the assumption that there are some universal characteristics of all females and all males that are located in their respective bodies, so the biological body is the ultimate basis of gender. It was precisely this view that feminist scholars were attempting to undermine by using the concept of gender.

Historians of science, however, have demonstrated that biological science, itself, is influenced by ideas about gender difference. Londa Schiebinger, for example, has shown that beliefs about gender in eighteenth-century Europe were crucial in shaping how scientists developed classificatory schemes and built scientific knowledge about plants and animals.[3] For example, using ideas about gender differences in human beings, plants were "sexed" and the breast was used as a means of distinguishing mammals from other animal species. As empirical knowledge based on the senses became the privileged source of truth, scientists began to search for the "real" difference between women and men. Eventually it became "common sense" that the "real" difference between all females and all males was the part their bodies played in reproduction. Genitalia, hormones, and chromosomes were understood to constitute the reality of sex difference, in spite of the many variations within the category "woman" and within the category "man" and regardless of the existence of human beings whose physiology and anatomy did not fit into either category. Babies born with ambiguous genitalia had to be surgically gendered to fit the idea of sex difference.

Science, under the influence of political and cultural ideas about gender (and race), interpreted "nature," and then this culturally influenced scientific knowledge was used to justify the belief in "natural" differences. Most of us are so accustomed to looking to science/nature/biology as the ultimate source of truth, especially when it concerns bodies, that it is difficult to think outside of this framework. But historical scholarship helps us to do just that.

Importantly, Thomas Laqueur, examining numerous sources, including medical texts and anatomical drawings of the human body beginning with ancient Greece, discovered that before the Enlightenment, that is, prior to the eighteenth century, male and female bodies were viewed as similar, and what he calls a "one-sex" model of the body dominated scientific and philosophical understanding.[4] There was but one body, a male body, and females were thought to have the same organs as males, but theirs were inside their bodies rather than outside of them. Bodily fluids were understood to be interchangeable, such that blood, milk, fat, and semen could turn into one another. Laqueur shows that historically even the major figures of the Renaissance scientific revolution assimilated their empirical observations to the cultural and political belief in the similarity of the sexes. This view of sex and the body was in accord with the idea that women were but inferior versions of men. It was not until the eighteenth century that the modern view that men and women were opposite sexes – they were different rather than similar – came to dominate how sex was understood. Scientists increasingly searched for, found, and gave names to the bodily indicators of an essential difference. Schiebinger has shown that eighteenth-century physicians sought and believed they had found the fundamental nature of sex in every part of the body – in blood vessels, sweat, brains, hair, and bones.[5]

The question of why there was a shift during the eighteenth century is still an open one. Laqueur argues forcefully that the answer does not lie in the advances in empirical science. He suggests that as a consequence of the Enlightenment, religion and metaphysics were displaced by science as the ultimate source of truth. With the political upheavals associated with the French Revolution that began to dismantle social hierarchies, including threatening the political privileges of men in contrast to women, the biological body came to be understood as the ultimate source of the differences in men's and women's social and political capacities. Another factor contributing to efforts to demarcate bodily difference is likely to have been a consequence of European imperial expansion, with the discovery of ever more varieties of plants, animals, and, especially, other groups of human beings. Although arguments about the existence of a "one-sex" model and the dating of the transformation in scientific views of bodily difference have not gone unchallenged, the idea that culture, in this case ideas about gender, has shaped knowledge about sex and the body has become widely accepted.[6]

While Laqueur and Schiebinger have demonstrated the consequences of gender, or the historically changing beliefs about sexual difference for scientific understandings of sex and the body, philosopher Judith Butler has elaborated a way of understanding sex and the body that dismantles the widely assumed opposition between "nature" and culture.[7] She has developed a complex set of ideas arguing that sex is a cultural achievement with bodily (material) consequences. If gender is the cultural construction of sex, then sex and the body are the effects of or are produced by discourse. This does not mean, according to Butler, that sex and the body are imagined or are somehow invented by language. Rather, she argues that the body itself becomes gendered through repeated bodily acts, a process that she terms "performativity." Gender, in other words, becomes embodied, and what we think of as sex is the effect of this "reiterative" or ritual practice – a practice that results in sex being seen as totally "natural." The sociologist Raewyn Connell puts a similar conceptualization differently. She argues that gender "norms" have physical effects on the body. Gender becomes incorporated into the body in practice – in acting and interacting in the social world. "The forms and consequences of this incorporation change in time, and change as a result of social purposes and social struggle. That is to say they are fully historical.... in the reality of practice the body is never outside history, and history never free of bodily presence and effects on the body."[8] She argues, for example, that "the physical sense of maleness grows through a personal history of social practice, a life-history-in-society."[9] Philosophers such as Elizabeth Grosz, as well as feminist biologists, have developed ways of thinking about bodies that understand them not as fixed, but rather as always in states of becoming.[10] Such ways of thinking are important because they break down the dichotomy between the material and the cultural, between sex and gender, and make possible not only histories of gender, but histories of the body using gender as a tool of historical analysis.

What might a history of the body focus upon using gender as a category of historical analysis? Feminist medical historians have studied the changing medical practices on and beliefs about the female body. Bodies also have been at issue in histories of birth control and pro-natalist movements as well as in campaigns against venereal disease. As Kathleen Canning has demonstrated, bodies have been central to women's political activism, as, for example, when female textile workers in Weimar Germany during the mid-1920s organized to demand that the state expand maternity protections.[11] Histories of the body or bodies in history also have concerned men's bodies at war. Joanna Bourke, for example, has examined the impact of World War I on men's bodies.[12] She explores how those who returned maimed from the Front dealt with their disabilities, and analyzes how the impact of the conflict shaped post-war masculinity. Other scholars also have examined the historical links that have been made between the health and welfare of individual bodies and the society at large, understood as the "social body."[13]

Carolyn Walker Bynum's *Holy Feast and Holy Fast: The Religious Significance of Food to Medieval Women* was one of the earliest and most important studies that made gender and the body historically central.[14] As its title suggests, the book concerns European Christian women between 1200 and 1500 and the association between their religious devotion and food. Medieval women used the symbol of denying themselves food (during a time of food scarcity) and bringing pain upon themselves to more closely associate themselves with Christ's suffering on the cross, while through the communion wafer they ingested the body of God. Bynum argued that their asceticism that took the form of self-torture was an effort to use their bodily senses to get closer to God.

Historical analyses of the period of the French Revolution have been especially important in showing the symbolic significance of bodies as sites of political meaning. Dorinda Outram's study, for example, suggests that particularly at such a time of complex social and political transformation, bodies become important signifiers of political allegiance and of political standing. To illustrate this, she argues that the depiction of heroic masculinity derived from Greek Stoic classical antiquity served to validate the political participation of men while denigrating and excluding women from politics.[15] Lynn Hunt's work has also shown the significance of the body in the political and social transformations associated with the Revolution. She suggests, for example, that the period witnessed great anxiety about social differentiation, and as a consequence increasing attention was paid to how bodies were clothed and what that clothing said about the wearers' loyalty to revolutionary ideals. In the *ancien régime*, ornate men's clothing signified privilege and aristocratic power, and the elegance of their dress was at least as prominent as was female finery. After the Revolution, men disposed of their stockings, high heels, wigs, and pantaloons, replacing them with a more "uniform uniform."[16] What mattered now was their similarity to one another and their difference from women.

Isabel Hull's analysis of the development of civil society in Germany during the eighteenth and early nineteenth centuries suggests that as men were to enter the public sphere and engage in civil society as individuals rather than as members of particular families, professions, estates, or religions, "they thought of themselves in some important sense as naked."[17] They, too, had shed the signs of their difference from one another and, as in France, their bodily difference from women defined a man's identity.

Analyses of the practices of the veiling of women and of reactions to the veil also suggest the significance of bodily representation for national and/or ethnic identity. In his study of Central Asia, *Veiled Empire*, Douglas Northrop has revealed that before the 1917 Bolshevik Revolution, while Central Asian women and men engaged in practices that were deeply gendered, there was fluidity and variability in those practices and in how gender difference was represented.[18] It was only after the advent of Russian colonial control and especially after the Revolution that particular forms of female dress and female seclusion came to be deemed traditional. The veil and seclusion were used as national symbols *encouraged* by the Soviets, who, for a time, believed that the existence of an indigenous nation such as Uzbekistan in Central Asia could represent Soviet modernity. By the mid-1920s, the party line changed and the practices of female veiling and seclusion were denounced as dirty and oppressive and an indicator that the Uzbeks were incapable of civilization. In 1927, the Soviets insisted on unveiling women in order to transform Uzbek society. Uzbeks who opposed the Soviet campaign of unveiling then portrayed themselves as defenders of the nation by insisting on the veil. Both the Soviets and Uzbek nationalists used women's veiled bodies as pawns in the conflict between them.

In her analysis of the contemporary "headscarf" controversy in France, Joan Scott suggests that a major reason that the veil has become so contested is as a consequence of the mismatch between two distinctive ways of dealing with the issue of sexual difference.[19] For Islam the veil announces a limit to male–female interaction, declaring sexual exchanges in public to be "off-limits." Veiling and the headscarf make visible and explicit anxieties about sexuality and sex difference. In contrast the French deny that sex difference is and has been politically salient by conspicuously displaying women's bodies, to represent the French gender system as superior, free, and "natural." Muslims' attitudes to sex and sexuality are then thought by the French to make them unassimilable.

Scott's analysis of the contemporary discord over veiled women in France and some of the other works noted above are simultaneously concerned with bodily practices and beliefs about sexuality. Another example of the close association between images of the body and issues of sexuality is to be found in the work of Iranian historian Afsaneh Najmabadi.[20] She has written about the changing ideals of beauty over the nineteenth and early twentieth centuries. Using paintings among other sources, she shows that ideals of beauty were not distinguished by gender in the late eighteenth century and early nineteenth centuries. The beauty of males and females was described similarly in texts while they were depicted in paintings with corresponding features and shapes. Over the course of the nineteenth century, however, ideas about beauty became increasingly differentiated by gender. These changes were associated with changing ideas about sexuality, especially the nature of male eroticism. Early in the nineteenth century, young men could be objects of beauty and sexual desire, as were young women. The distinction between male and female forms of beauty and ideas about male sexuality developed over the century as a consequence of the rise of the modern nation-state and in the context of European contact.

As this example makes clear, the history of the body as a field shares some of its purview with the history of sexuality, and as Najmabadi's work and Scott's analysis show, the two often are inextricably connected. But sexuality need not necessarily be the focus of body histories. Histories of the body generally concern how bodies are represented and serve as symbols, how they are shaped through various organized social practices, and how they become the focus of political mobilization.

As a field of study, however, histories of sexuality are particularly concerned with the various histories of the regulation and control of erotic practices, the categories naming, interpreting, and classifying them and the range of consequences of societal concern about sexual desire and activity, including the creation of sexual identities. As Raewyn Connell has argued, sexual categories and norms as well as the forms and objects of desire, "the patterning of sexuality through the life history, the practices through which pleasure is given and received, all differ between cultures and are subject to transformation in time."[21] Prostitution, same-sex relationships, population control by the state, birth control, attitudes toward marital and non-marital intimacy, understandings of men and women as sexual beings, are included in histories of sexuality and most incorporate gender as a category of historical analysis.

The contemporary field of the history of sexuality was influenced by developments in women's history and feminist history more generally as well as the rise of gay and lesbian rights movements, and it was profoundly stimulated by the publication of Michel Foucault's *History of Sexuality*, published in the late 1970s.[22] Importantly, Foucault maintained that the efforts at controlling sexuality in Western society beginning in the nineteenth century were not repressive, as had commonly been thought. Rather, the avid attention to sex in the discourses of science as well as popular literature about it served as incitements to speak and think about sexual desire. Foucault maintained that modern discourses of sexuality were a dispersed form of power that created not only desire, but also identities, so that who we are is defined by our sexual practices. In fact, the very term "sexuality" was created through these discourses.

Elaborating on Foucault's views, in his historical overview of the history of sexuality in modern Europe, Jeffrey Weeks argues that

> as society has become more and more concerned with the lives of its members, for the sake of moral uniformity, economic well-being, national security or hygiene and health, so it has become more and more preoccupied with the sex lives of its individuals, giving rise to intricate methods of administration and management, to a flowering of moral anxieties, medical hygienic, legal and welfarist interventions, or scientific delving, *all designed to understand the self by understanding sex.*[23]

It is precisely the connection between sexuality and the self that was central in Foucault's ideas about modern sexuality and how modern understandings of sexuality differed from understandings of sex in ancient and pre-modern Europe and in Asia as well.

Historians now understand that the homosexual is a modern category that did not exist before the nineteenth century. Even before the publication of Foucault's work, lesbian and gay historians were suggesting that the heterosexual–homosexual dichotomy was of recent provenance. While earlier European societies were concerned to regulate sexual practices in the interests of reproduction and inheritance, homosexuality as it is understood today, as a presumed state of being that defines the identities of people who engage in same-sex intimacies, would have made no sense in the past.

Same-sex erotic activity surely existed in all cultures, but those who engaged in it were not seen as homosexuals. Historical research concerning same-sex activity in the past helps to make clear the historicity of sexuality and how it was regulated.

The historian of the ancient world David Halperin has argued, based on his research, that in ancient Athens sexual partners were not understood as males or females but rather as dominant and submissive; active and passive; penetrator and penetrated.[24] These were not taken as signs of some sort of sexual identity. Rather, the practices were understood as expressions of personal status and indicated one's social but not sexual identity. Halperin uses the analogy of burglary to make clear how sexual activity would have been understood. Sexual engagement was not seen in the ancient world as a mutual act any more than we understand that the burglar and the victim engage in a mutual and voluntary act. Male citizens of Athens could penetrate those who were of lesser status, including boys, women, slaves, and foreigners. There are examples from across the world and over time of age differences structuring sexual relations, including in seventeenth-century Japan.[25]

In medieval and early modern Europe the practice of same-sex erotic behavior was known as sodomy, although the term also could refer to a variety of other forms of behavior considered deviant. Helmut Puff has explored the changing discourses and regimes of control of sodomy in certain German-speaking areas of Europe during the period from the fifteenth to the seventeenth centuries.[26] Basing his analysis on a range of texts, including trials and literary and religious writings, he showed that women as well as men could be accused of sodomy. Earlier, in the middle ages, sodomy had been associated with religious heresy, and those accused would be executed. In the early years of the Protestant Reformation there were extensive efforts to rid cities of sexual offenders, and religious sermons and tracts contributed to an extensive discourse on sodomy that urged people to live their lives free of sin. Protestant reformers frequently accused Catholic leaders of sodomy and portrayed the practice as the brutish contrast to marriage. During the period of the Protestant and Catholic reforms of the sixteenth century, authorities increasingly attempted to restrict what was said about sodomy, but at the same time in Zurich and Lucerne there were sexual cultures in which male same-sex activity was common.

Across Europe in the context of religious and political turmoil in the period from the sixteenth through to the eighteenth centuries, what was perceived to be sexual deviance was harshly punished and subject to surveillance. The Catholic Church in Spain and Italy during the Inquisition harshly punished those believed to be sexually immoral, and the Church made clear that procreative sex sanctified by marriage was the only form of sexuality that would be permitted. Protestants both in Europe and in North America, likewise, severely punished prostitutes and adulterers and burned at the stake those accused of sodomy. Around the turn of the eighteenth century, for example, the Netherlands executed hundreds of people accused of sodomy.[27]

Randolph Trumbach's research on the period in English history from the 1680s to the 1790s reveals that during the eighteenth century there was a transformation in the sexual identities of men.[28] Before then, sexual activities between men in young adulthood probably were fairly common, but they did not mark men's identities in any discernible way. During the first decades of the eighteenth century, however, male sexual practices came to be seen as either exclusively heterosexual activity or sodomy. London was seen as being populated by men, women, and "sodomites." "Sodomites," thus, constituted a "third gender." A thriving subculture of men who engaged in same-sex activity existed in eighteenth-century London, where men who desired sex with other men congregated in what was known as "molly houses"; men thought to be frequenting them were in turn defamed as "mollies." In order to prove their masculinity, men of all classes had to comply with the new heterosexual sexual order. Accompanying this transformation of normative sexuality with its concurrent emphasis on domesticity and family life, there was a rise in extramarital sex, which was sanctioned for men but not women, as well as a rise in prostitution. Prostitutes served men not only as commercialized sexual objects, but also as resources for securing their heterosexual reputations. Female prostitutes and male sodomites were similarly denigrated. Trumbach's research should not be understood as constructing a "golden age" of sexual freedom versus sexual restraint. Rather, he is concerned to trace the increasing emphasis on heterosexuality as a crucial component of manliness, defined in contrast to those "others" seen as "sodomites" who participated in a visible same-sex subculture.

George Chauncey's important study of male–male sexuality and sexual subcultures in four areas of New York City, *Gay New York*, describes and analyzes a period around the turn of the twentieth century when men from a variety of walks of life openly thwarted societal norms of exclusive heterosexuality, participating in a lively and complex gay world.[29] It was during this time that the terms "homosexual" and "heterosexual" appeared. A gay subculture emerged first in the 1890s in an area known as the Bowery, where working-class immigrants lived and a red-light district flourished. There, men who desired men, defined by medical and other experts at the time as "inverts," but known locally as "fairies," adopted exaggerated feminine modes of behaviour in public. The "respectable middle-class" men who secretly visited them from other areas of the city, where involvement in same-sex activity would have destroyed their reputations, called themselves "queer." Fairy culture developed in bohemian Greenwich Village and black Harlem in the 1910s and 1920s. Class and race differences structured how men understood their acts and perceived their partners. Gay and sexually permissive cultures that included places of lesbian activity expanded during the years of (alcohol) Prohibition into central areas of the city. The repeal of Prohibition in 1931, however, witnessed the beginning of an intensive crusade of repression against gays and lesbians, who were now seen as degenerate, as contrasted with those people who led exclusively heterosexual lives of domesticity. Interestingly, Chauncey also tells us that the term "gay" first was used to refer to prostitutes, and they, like gay men were considered "perverts."

Although lesbians make a brief appearance in books by Trumbach and Chauncey, both focus primarily on men. Studying women's same-sex relationships has been troubled by the availability of sources and questions concerning how to interpret them. How are the sexual subjectivities of women in the past to be studied if their same-sex activities are not named; if the women do not identify themselves and their relationships with other women in terms that are understandable to us as sexual references?

Martha Vicinus has suggested that women's sexual subjectivities are and have been fluid and that understanding women's same-sex relationships in the past involves seeing a "continuum of women's sexual behaviors, in which lesbian sexuality can be both a part of and apart from normative heterosexual marriage and child-bearing."[30] She argues that neither the visibility of women's intimate relations with other women nor names or labels for those relationships are necessary in order to comprehend women's sexual identities or subjectivities in the past.[31] These ideas are illuminated in her study, *Intimate Friends: Women Who Loved Women, 1778–1928.*[32] This work explores various instances of educated middle- and upper-class Anglo-American women's same-sex intimate relationships over the period using women's words about themselves gleaned from diaries, letters, and court testimony as well as fiction and poetry. These sources are mined to reveal how women represented the passionate and erotic affection they shared with one another. Vicinus discusses, for example, how some women who had erotic attachments to other women made use of the Victorian vision of sexually pure womanhood to reject and abstain from heterosexual sex. She documents relationships between women who lived with one another as married partners, such as the Ladies of Llangollen (Sarah Ponsonby and Eleanor Butler), and details the intrigues of the community of American and British women living in mid-nineteenth-century Rome, some of whom moved in and out of heterosexual relationships as well as forming same-sex marriages with one another. Her cases include women who adopted mannish modes of self-presentation, portraying themselves as tomboyish, "rakish," or gentlemanly, but did so fluidly such that the self-styled rake might become a protective husband or the tomboy a prudent mother. One of the cases involved two women who, in 1809, ran a boarding school and apparently there shared a bed. They initiated a libel trial against an aristocratic woman whose Anglo-Indian grandchild, a student at the school, accused the schoolmistresses of "indecent and criminal practices." They won the libel case on the "racial" grounds that such behavior was not known to take place among British women and thus their indecency was a figment of the distorted imagination of the colonial "half-caste" child. The accused women, nevertheless, were hounded from the school. The cases that Vicinus examines over a 150-year period reveal a variety of ways that women engaged in and understood their erotic and loving relations with one another and crafted their own identities.

Basing their study on oral histories of working-class lesbians in Buffalo, New York, who lived and formed same-sex relationships in the post-World War II years, Elizabeth Lapovsky Kennedy and Madeline D. Davis explored the creation of the sexual subjectivities of the women and the development of their lesbian identities and group consciousness.[33] These working-class women created a "butch–fem" culture that visibly announced their erotic difference as a way of confronting the outside world. They manipulated symbols of heterosexual monogamy as a way to refuse to abide by the norms of the larger society and to defend their right to same-sex relationships. The authors argue that these "tough bar lesbians" resisted male dominance and normative heterosexuality and defended themselves against public harassment using bar rooms that they defined as their preserve through their gendered role-playing.

Anxieties about masturbation also have been studied by historians. Isabel Hull's discussion of sexuality in Germany's "long eighteenth century," referred to earlier with regard to histories of the body, includes an examination of the outpouring of anti-masturbation literature in the 1780s.[34] The main assumption of that literature, which focused on males, was that semen, understood as the source of masculine strength, would be lost as a result of the practice, leading to both physical and mental weakness. The discourse about masturbation associated the practice with overly civilized living, especially in cities. Boarding schools as well as servants were blamed for introducing children to the practice. They also were supposed to have learned it from reading, and were made susceptible because of new kinds of associations and forms of sociability. Hull suggests that anxiety about masturbation and the belief that the habit had increased was a consequence of fears about the material, social, and cultural changes of the time and how they affected children and youth.

Like same-sex and solitary sex, prostitution, too, has histories. How prostitutes were viewed, how prostitution was organized and regulated, and, as we saw in Trumbach's work discussed above, prostitution's role in educating or confirming masculinity and male sexuality in different time periods and cultural settings all have been the object of scholarship.

Ruth Mazo Karras' study of prostitution in medieval England, based on a range of source materials, including sermons, civic rules regulating brothels, church and secular court records, examines how prostitutes were viewed, and the economic, social, and cultural conditions under which they lived. While prostitutes, themselves, were maligned, the practice of prostitution was tolerated as a "necessary evil." Although town brothels did not commonly exist in England as they did in medieval Germany and elsewhere on the Continent, Southampton and Sandwich maintained legal brothels, apparently to provide for the needs of sailors in order to safeguard the virtue of the towns' respectable wives and daughters. Karras argues that women's sexual behavior, generally, was a subject of gossip and public attention, as it defined their reputations in the communities in which they lived. Respectable married women were believed capable of becoming "common women," and thus they, too, needed to be controlled and supervised. The sin of lust was believed to characterize all women, but it was the whore who "acted on that lust indiscriminately."[35]

In late medieval Augsburg, as Lyndal Roper has shown, brothels were municipally run services designed especially for youth as a kind of apprenticeship for manhood and marriage. Roper argues that prostitution reinforced male bonding and "defined sexual virility as an essential male characteristic."[36] But respectable women, too, were thought to benefit from prostitution because the practice afforded them safety. Virginity was highly prized just as it was in marriage, and a man's masculinity was especially confirmed if he was the first to penetrate a particular woman. As a consequence of urging by Lutheran preachers, the brothels were made illegal in 1532. The Lutherans encouraged the belief that men's sexual natures were controllable, and that their sexual desires could be channeled into matrimony. But with the new regime came greater powers of surveillance, and the boundary between the prostitute and non-prostitute became blurred. Women's sexual desires were feared and all women were suspected of being capable of debauchery.

Judith Walkowitz's important study of prostitution in Victorian England focuses on the campaign to repeal the Contagious Diseases Acts, which had been passed by Parliament in 1864.[37] Designed to protect soldiers and sailors from venereal disease, the Acts authorized police in garrison towns to require women suspected of prostitution to register as prostitutes and to undergo a humiliating medical examination. If women who were suspected of prostitution were found to be infected with disease, they faced long jail sentences. The Ladies National Association (LNA), under the leadership of Josephine Butler, opposed the Acts on the grounds that not only were they ineffective in stopping the spread of venereal disease, but they punished the women but not the men who used them and whom the LNA accused of being the cause of the vice and its consequences. Walkowitz's work reveals not only the work of the middle-class philanthropically minded members of the LNA, but also their complicated relationships and interactions with the prostitutes, whom they attempted to rescue and in whose name they fought against the Acts. They portrayed themselves sometimes as sisters who understood that poverty could lead any woman to choose prostitution, but also as "mothers" who saw the prostitutes as passive figures who had lost their innocence but whose virtue could be restored in rescue homes. Walkowitz's *Prostitution and Victorian Society* also opens a window onto the lives of poor women, showing that the women who registered as prostitutes under the Acts were similar in almost all respects to other young women living in their neighborhoods. They did not think of themselves as prostitutes, and usually left lives as sex workers in their late twenties either to cohabit with a man or for marriage. One of the effects of the Acts, Walkowitz demonstrates, is that the average age of the women who registered as prostitutes rose and prostitution increasingly became a career rather than a temporary way of making a living. The Acts were finally repealed in 1886.

As it happens, anxiety about venereal disease was if anything more pervasive in the British Empire than in the metropole: contagious diseases acts were passed overseas before
they were passed at home and they involved greater levels of
surveillance. Philippa Levine's exhaustive study of prostitution in the British Empire during and after the period of the
metropolitan contagious diseases acts and the movement for
their abolition (1860–1918) examines the intersection of
gender, race, and concerns about imperial governance in the
regulation of prostitution.[38] The practice of prostitution by
colonial subjects was regarded by the imperial government as
an indication of their immorality and lack of civilization but
deemed a necessary evil when the clients were European.
Prostitution was regulated to protect these clients not the
local population. The East, especially, was regarded as a site
of sexual licentiousness, and prostitution was often regarded
as evidence for the necessity of colonialism. Yet, colonial
officials argued that prostitution was essential as an outlet
for aggressive male sexuality believed characteristic of soldiers and imperial men. In various parts of the Empire, military and civilian colonial authorities classified brothels
according to the "race" of the clients frequenting them. First-
class brothels served only white men, and in India, where
European women worked in brothels, those, too, were considered first-class and were restricted to British soldiers.
Third-class brothels were for local clients and providers.
Unlike in the metropole, brothels were legalized and regulated. In Southeast Asian colonies, prostitutes were required
to carry identity cards, and by the end of the nineteenth
century, their photographs and the details about them had to
be displayed at the brothel.

The regulation of prostitution in the interests of the military was not only a feature of Victorian Britain until the
mid-1880s and in the British Empire for a longer time period,
but it also became policy in Nazi Germany, as research by
Annette Timm has shown.[39] When the Nazis first came to
power they used the authority of the law to define prostitution and sexual activity with Jews as "asocial" and subject
to punishment. They engaged in a strenuous effort to "clean
up the streets," subjecting streetwalkers to strict penalties.
However, many city administrators instituted brothels, insist-

ing that they were necessary to protect public health. From the mid-1930s state-sponsored brothels were legitimated by the government and promoted by the military. Prostitutes themselves, however, were denigrated as "racially inferior," although their availability in brothels was seen to serve both hygienic and military functions. With the beginning of the war, women who were considered prostitutes were registered and restricted to brothels. If they left police and medical control they were sent to concentration camps. Women who frequented bars and other places of entertainment were subject to intensifying surveillance, and all public displays of female sexuality were seen as threatening the health of the population. At the same time both military and civilian brothels became increasingly available. Timm argues that public health ultimately was not the reason for the institutionalization of prostitution. Rather, protection against venereal disease was a "smokescreen" for the state's concern to channel sexuality to the needs of its aggressive militarism and racial policies. Men could only be men and virile, effective soldiers if they were sexually satisfied and given the opportunity to perform masculine sexuality. Male sexuality and the nation's military strength mirrored each other.

Conclusion

This chapter has covered questions concerning the sex/gender dichotomy and reviewed arguments suggesting that biology and the notion of biological sex itself have a history. It has discussed ways of thinking that retain some sort of notion of the material body while not assuming that the body is outside of culture. The chapter has also explored some of the historical studies that center on bodies and on sexuality using gender as a category of analysis. How might we summarize some of the ways that gender is critical both to histories of the body and to histories of sexuality? We have seen that the gendered bodies of both males and females and their sexual activities have been deployed as political symbols or symbols of the nation. In the late eighteenth century, gender difference as indicated by dress appears to have become critical in establishing men's similarity to one another and difference from women in France during the Revolution and in Germany with the development of civil society. How gender difference was marked on the body of women became central to the Soviet regime in Central Asia and then became a focus of nationalist opposition to the regime. We have learned that while there have been historical changes in how same-sex sexual practices were viewed, anxiety about and hostility to same-sex sexual activity were associated with religious insistence upon marital procreative sex. While tolerance of same-sex sexual practices varied historically, sexual identities appear to have originated during the eighteenth and nineteenth centuries. And we have learned that both men who engaged in same-sex interactions and women who sexually desired other women often adopted gendered personae and might subvert society's gender norms in their pursuit of same-sex erotic relationships. Finally, we have seen that the regulation of prostitution was not only due to anxieties about female sexuality, but also was related to particular understandings of masculinity and male sexuality and the "race" of the men and women involved. The next chapter will explore the argument that race/ethnicity, class, and gender are not independent dimensions of social life, but rather they are relationally constituted and intersect in historically important ways.

3
Gender and Other Relations of Difference

As Chapter 1 mentioned all too briefly, one of the major critiques of 1970s and 1980s women's history was that it ignored differences among women. Over the course of the 1980s, black and Latina feminist scholars questioned what seemed to be a predominant emphasis in US women's history on white, middle-class women. As a consequence of their scholarship and criticism, the field of women's history became more inclusive. This trend fostered a great deal of reflection about how race and ethnic differences influenced the ways that gender affected women's lives. In their introduction to the first edition of *Unequal Sisters* published in 1990, US historians Vicki Ruiz and Ellen Carol DuBois wrote:

> Growing demands for the recognition of "difference" – the diversity of women's experiences can no longer be satisfied by token excursions in the histories of minority women....The journey into women's history itself has to be remapped. From many corners comes the call for a more complex approach to women's experiences, one that explores not only the conflicts between women and men but also the conflicts among women; not only the bonds among women but also the bonds between women and men. Only such a multifaceted perspective will be sufficient "to illuminate the interconnections among the various systems of power that shape women's lives."[1]

The challenge, they recognized, was to keep race, class, and gender "equally and simultaneously in play" in order to produce a more complete history of women's lives.[2]

The field of gender history developed within this context as feminist scholars increasingly recognized that gender, understood as a hierarchical ordering of the relations between women and men and/or as the meanings given to perceived differences between them, did not operate in the same way for all women and men in a particular historical moment. Rather, it became increasingly apparent that how gender played out in the lives of women and men, and the very meanings of "woman" and "man," depended upon other hierarchically ordered differences as well as differences across cultures. Thus, gender does not have a history but rather it has histories.

One of the important aspects of gender history as a field of feminist scholarship is its focus on context. A primary question that interested some gender historians was a crucial one: how was gender difference constructed and understood given contexts in which class and/or race/ethnicity also operated to create relationships of unequal power? Answers to such a question involve not only recognizing diversity both across cultures and within a given society, but also seeing how relationships among women and among men as well as between them are affected by complexly formed differences in power. They also involve examining how gender may have been complicit in constructing other differences and hierarchical arrangements.

To investigate how gender has been lived in different times and places and to interrogate how gender differences have been constructed, the concept needs to be understood relationally. As Gisela Bock wrote in 1989, "Looking at gender as a sociocultural relation enables us to see the links between gender and numerous other sociocultural relations in a fresh light....gender is one constituent factor of all other relations."[3] To study how gender and race/ethnicity and/or class have been mutually constituted and have worked together historically, scholars have had to focus on the contact between groups, whether that contact existed in the form of interpersonal relationships or via representations of "others."

Studies of women's and men's philanthropic and political activities illustrate the complex relations of gender, race/ ethnicity, and class. From the early 1970s, US women's historians had been interested in exploring and understanding white, middle-class women's philanthropic and welfare activities from the perspective of the separation of women and men into domestic and public spheres. Women who entered the public arena in the nineteenth and early twentieth centuries drew upon notions of womanhood to legitimate their participation in organizations promulgating policies and engaging in activities to help those less fortunate than themselves. But these ideals were not the same for all women. Linda Gordon's study comparing the welfare ideas of white and black women reformers in the early twentieth century revealed some important differences in the orientation of the two groups.[4] White women understood their welfare efforts as helping those who were not only socially, but also ethnically and religiously "other." Black women in contrast saw themselves as helping "their own kind," although the reformers were more economically privileged and better educated than the intended welfare recipients. Gordon's comparison of the orientations of black and white women suggests that white women social workers saw themselves dispensing charity or relief while black women, who often lived in the same or similar neighborhoods as their clients, concentrated more on education and health. They sought to provide universal services, in contrast to white reformers, who supported welfare programs that were means-tested and which made moral distinctions between those who were worthy of help and those who were not. While the concerns of black and white reformers were to a certain extent shaped by their shared understandings of gender, Gordon shows that "race" mattered to their different visions of welfare.

Nancy Hewitt's study of Latina women's philanthropic activity in nineteenth-century Tampa, Florida, suggested that social class differentiated how co-ethnic Latina women viewed these endeavors. Affluent Spanish women saw their volunteer work as charity, whereas working-class Cuban women talked about mutual aid. Hewitt concluded that her study of forms of philanthropy in Tampa shows "the intricate interdependency of individuals' class, ethnic, and gender identities and experiences."[5]

In late nineteenth-century London, women from the middle and upper classes regularly went into poor neighborhoods as home visitors, as Ellen Ross has shown. In the early twentieth century they gave instruction on baby care and delousing children, and questioned their clients about the nature of the jobs their 12- to 14-year-old children were taking. "Ladies" who were health visitors and social workers came into the homes of working-class mothers and attempted to "modernize" their methods of feeding and childcare, which they saw as outmoded and deleterious, having been learned from "old gamps and dowagers" in their neighborhoods.[6] Ross, however, maintains that the "ladies" were not just patronizing benefactors. Rather, some of them also showed insight into and empathy with the women who were their clients.

In her study of the influence of white, middle-class reformers on early twentieth-century US welfare policy, Gwendolyn Mink has argued that the policies that they promoted supported motherhood, but that those who implemented them coupled support for motherhood with a particular vision about how immigrant women ought to be mothers. What Mink and other scholars have termed "maternalist" policies defined ethnic motherhood as "other" to "American" motherhood, and thus counter to the interests of the larger public. Educators stressed "Americanization" of girls through teaching homemaking and cooking in schools. Visiting teachers taught immigrant mothers to substitute proper "American" ingredients for those with which they were familiar in their customary recipes. American cheese and butter were to be substituted for olive oil and parmesan cheese. Garlic was frowned upon, and women of Mexican origin in the southwest were taught to make butter and flour-based sauces instead of tomato sauces containing nuts, chilies, and cheese.[7]

While Mink's research included examples of how "Americanization" of motherhood was a significant aspect of the development and implementation of welfare policies in the early twentieth century, Nyan Shah has focused in some detail on how white, middle-class women in San Francisco in the last quarter of the nineteenth century were influenced in their projects of domestic reform by popular attitudes about the domestic practices and social conduct of immigrant Chinese women. She focuses, in particular on Dr Mary Sawtelle, a local physician and editor of a medical advice journal who maintained that Chinese women were prostitutes who "conspired to inoculate American families with syphilis," and on Presbyterian women missionaries who, like the white Victorian "ladies" of London, encouraged home visits in their efforts to reform the hygienic practices of married Chinese women. Sawtelle along with other physicians and the missionaries, Shah argues, envisioned white, middle-class household norms as opposite to the cultural practices of the Chinese. Their reform efforts were shaped by both a middle-class culture of domesticity with women as its guardians and the growing belief that bodily health was a civic duty. Furthermore, they focused their attention on "moral purity" as a gendered duty associated with white, American womanhood. Ironically, in the 1920s and 1930s, Chinese American social workers used the association between hygiene, domesticity, and gender, citing evidence to show that Chinatown had become the site of a flourishing "family society" to advocate for improved social services for their community.[8]

In her essay, Shah linked the women's projects of domestic reform in San Francisco with a broader imperial project involving Protestant missionaries' efforts to civilize "others" abroad by exporting their vision of middle-class domesticity. Middle-class domesticity, influenced by evangelical Protestantism in the early nineteenth century, also was important to British women's campaigns against slavery. Clare Midgley's *Women against Slavery: The British Campaigns, 1780–1870* argues that female abolitionists, building on their gendered identification as women and mothers, and influenced by the ideology of separate spheres, set at the heart of their anti-slavery vision the breaking up of black family life and the suffering of women brutally punished and sexually exploited as slaves. Midgley suggests that there is a connection between women's engagement in abolition and their philanthropic activities and evangelical missionary work in Britain. They saw their involvement as a "duty incumbent upon women in their assigned role as guardians of morality," and they combined a "belief in black humanity with a conviction of African cultural inferiority."[9] Although women's abolitionist organizations in the 1820s adopted the slogan, "Am I not a woman and a sister?" Midgley argues that the images that they reproduced of black slaves showed them as supplicants, kneeling to appeal for help while white British women were represented as imperial maternal figures such as Britannia, Justice, Liberty, or Queen Victoria.

Women's abolitionist activities in Britain were framed within a larger imperial project. So, too, was the work of the Baptist missionary men who went to the West Indian slave colony of Jamaica in the 1820s. As Catherine Hall has shown in her exhaustively researched book *Civilising Subjects: Metropole and Colony in the English Imagination 1830–1867*, the missionaries ardently opposed slavery because the system turned the white planters into sexual degenerates as well as denying enslaved women and men the benefits of family life. Young men who became missionaries underwent training designed to imbue them with the values of Christian manliness and they were expected to marry before beginning their missionary activities in Jamaica. Marriage was revered and thought necessary to the manliness of missionaries in part because it fostered their wives' domesticity and secured their own integrity. Family was crucial to the comfort of missionaries, who faced hostility from the planters because of their involvement with black people, and the "family enterprise" provided a model for their relationship with their congregations. "The missionary's role in the family enterprise was closely linked to his fatherhood – head of household, father of the family, father of the congregation, father of the children in 'his' schools."[10] Such a patriarchal system was structured by both a gender and a racial hierarchy. Missionaries saw their efforts as bringing "these 'poor creatures' to salvation, manhood and freedom."[11] They believed slaves to be helpless casualties of a despicable system. Hall argues, however, that racial hierarchy undercut their rhetoric of the equality of man, because the missionaries considered black people to be like children who were in need of their fatherly guidance.

Emancipation, they believed, would make former slaves independent. Then they would prosper, becoming like middle-class, white Englishmen exemplifying the values of

Christian manliness and maintaining their families. But the friendship between freed black slaves and missionaries had limits – limits that would not permit too much independence or tolerate behavior that did not conform to missionary ideals. Over time, missionaries in Jamaica and in England became disillusioned, and increasingly some of them came to believe that there was something "innate" about blacks that thwarted their becoming civilized Christians in the ways the missionaries had once imagined. The complexity of Hall's work showing how inextricably colony and metropole were joined cannot be fully appreciated in this brief discussion. But what is important for our purposes here is to see the many ways that race, combined with gender, was central to the abolitionist missionary enterprise, which itself was part of an imperial project.

In a ground-breaking study of British feminist periodicals and the literatures dealing with the campaign against the Contagious Diseases Acts in India as well as the suffrage campaign at home, Antoinette Burton showed the centrality of gender and imperial culture to nineteenth-century British feminist demands for political citizenship. Burton's contribution was important because it demonstrated how a British movement for women's rights in the metropole could only be fully comprehended by taking into account the imperial context within which feminists argued their worthiness for the vote. They did so, she demonstrates, by using the image of "the Indian woman" to argue that it was their gendered responsibility to participate in the "imperial civilizing mission." Burton's analysis shows how Indian women were represented as "helpless victims" who depended upon their British sisters in Britain to address their plight. Feminists focused on their degraded status as indicated by cultural practices such as child marriage, seclusion, and enforced widowhood. Feminist imperialism, in contrast to its masculinist counterpart, which stressed white men's military prowess, emphasized women's moral power as a necessary component of imperial power. Burton maintains that women's imperial mission was based on a sense of both Anglo-Saxon racial pride and British national self-esteem.[12]

A study of wealthy white women's philanthropic organizing in the West Indian colony of Barbados during the era of slavery and the decades immediately following emancipation illustrates some of the points about race, class, and gender detailed in the preceding paragraphs. Melanie Newton's "Philanthropy, Gender, and the Production of Public Life in Barbados, ca 1790–ca 1850," takes as its focus the struggle of the white elite to assert authority over free women and men of color and thereby reinforce a white/black racial hierarchy on the island. From the 1820s philanthropic organizations became active in Barbados. Some of them were sites where wealthy white women assumed a public maternal role; others were composed of free non-white men and women who deployed the ideology of domesticity to demonstrate their respectability and their place in the public sphere. While non-white philanthropic associations challenged the tenets of slavery and were used by free black elite men to make claims for political rights, white women's philanthropic efforts assisted the efforts of elite white men in reinforcing racial hierarchy.[13] As the earlier discussion of philanthropy also showed, white, elite women in Barbados pointed to the differences in the ways that gender shaped "other" women's domestic lives as a way of marking their own superiority over those "others." Gender relations and ideals of femininity often were imagined by elites to signify who could be thought to be civilized or to merit national belonging.

The work discussed so far suggests that while beneficent activities including philanthropy, abolitionism, and the defense of Indian women undoubtedly were well intentioned, and could have positive consequences for those "others" who were their recipients, such efforts were complexly configured and had multifaceted outcomes. These gendered humanitarian endeavors were shaped by "race" and/or class, relying on a hierarchical distinction between "us" and "them," and they served to construct or reinforce the particular class-, race-, and gender-based identities of the participants in them. Did such actors as Burton's feminists or Newton's Barbadian elites consciously and willfully manipulate ideologies involving gender, race, and class, and did they pursue them purposefully in order to make political claims or secure their own place in the society? Motivation is notoriously difficult to document. But we don't need to think in terms of individual motivations to understand how ideas about difference operate.

Rather, it is important to understand that the women and men involved in such activities spoke and acted in ways influenced by what was taken-for-granted at the time. In other words they were involved in activities that were part of larger class and/or imperial projects – projects that shaped how people understood themselves and the world around them. At the same time their words and actions were not only influenced by but contributed to the hierarchies of difference then at work.

The brief synopsis above of Newton's essay on free blacks and elite whites in the West Indies serves as a bridge to the discussion to follow of the enormously important scholarship on the role of the intersection of gender and race/ethnicity in slavery in the United States and the Caribbean and in imperial or colonial projects more generally. Of course the slave trade and the plantation slave system were central to British imperial projects in the Caribbean and, before the American Revolution, in North America. Furthermore, as Catherine Hall has underlined, the "time of empire was the time when anatomies of difference were elaborated across the axes of class, race and gender."[14] My discussion of the interdependence of gender and race in histories of slavery and colonialism will consider them separately, however, to indicate some of the different kinds of questions about them that gender historians have addressed.

Deborah Gray White's *Ar'n't I a Woman?*, published in 1979, and Jacqueline Jones' *Labor of Love, Labor of Sorrow*, published in 1985, were ground-breaking studies of black women's lives in slavery in the United States. White's book focused on women's lives and communities, but also explored their relationships with enslaved men. Her work suggests that relationships were relatively egalitarian, unlike the patriarchal families of the plantation owners. She shows that although there may have been a sexual division of labor within their households, this did not translate into one in which either men or women dominated their families.[15] Jones' work was an extensive study of women's lives in slavery and how the plantation system shaped the division of labor by sex, as well as its longer-term consequences for women's work and family relationships in post-emancipation society. Her book highlighted how slavery and its aftermath shaped the meanings of gender difference, and demonstrated the importance of taking into account how race and class differences inform the ways gender shapes people's lives. It made clear the differences between the gender relations and family lives of white elites and those they enslaved.[16] Historical studies by scholars such as White and Jones were important in demonstrating the differences among women and showing the gendered impact of slavery on women's work and family lives. More recent studies of gender and slavery, meanwhile, have gone beyond concern about the differences among women, women's status within their households, and the sexual division of labor to address the uses of gender for constructing racial categories, how gender and race together combined in the creation and management of slavery, and the centrality of gender as well as race to the slave system itself.

A premier example is Kathleen Brown's 1996 study, *Good Wives, Nasty Wenches and Anxious Patriarchs: Gender, Race and Power in Colonial Virginia*. Brown's book, using a variety of different kinds of evidence but especially legal records, carefully demonstrates the role of gender in the structuring of racial slavery in Virginia, England's first North American colony. Furthermore, the author shows how gender was critical to the construction of racial categories. Her analysis of how gender relations within the family and in the polity became transformed with the rise of slavery demonstrates the centrality of race to patriarchal gender relations.

Brown's work places gender at the very center of an historical narrative about colonial Virginia from the early seventeenth century to the middle of the eighteenth century and treats "gender, slavery and elite dominance as interrelated relationships of power whose histories intersect and mutually shape one another."[17] In other words Brown conceptualizes "race, class, and gender as overlapping and related social categories."[18]

The book's title captures a sense of the story that she tells. In early modern England the distinction between "good wives" and "nasty wenches" was meant to distinguish between "respectable" married women of England's "middling order" and poor English women suspected of being sexually licentious. Over the course of the seventeenth century in Virginia and with the growth of the tobacco economy, the distinction assumed new meanings. Early in the 1620s, English women were brought to the colony as indentured servants and worked alongside men in the fields. The distinction between "good wives" and "nasty wenches" came to mean "moral and respectable women – married and domestically employed – and depraved, degenerate wenches who were barely fit for the manual labor of men."[19] Marriage was critical to this distinction because it was through marriage that women could become "good wives" and their sexuality was brought under the control of their husbands. The distinction between "good wives" and "nasty wenches" was, thus, one of gender and marital status and social standing or class power. Over time, the distinction became racialized. Women of English descent were thought to be moral and virtuous while African-origin women were wenches who were assumed to be sexually licentious and capable of evil.

Brown demonstrates this shift by examining court cases and the creation of laws regulating slavery. In 1643 the Virginia Assembly passed a law distinguishing between English and enslaved African women who labored in the fields by making slave women "tithable" or taxable along with all employed English men and male slaves. African women, then, were legally understood as equivalent to male laborers, differentiating them from all English women. Thus womanhood became less a matter of class and increasingly one of race. Over the course of the 1660s other laws were passed that underscored the "racial" definition of slavery, separating Africans from others. In 1662 a statute defined the children born to enslaved African mothers as the property of their masters. Thus, regardless of who fathered the children, slavery became hereditary through African women. By 1668 free African women also had been declared tithable, further underscoring the idea that Africans were property, not persons. Laws such as these, focusing on African women, made the concept of "womanhood" itself race-specific. Finally, the prohibition on interracial marriage at the end of the seventeenth century gave white men exclusive sexual rights over white women, permitted harsh treatment of white female servants who slept with black men, and preserved white men's sexual access to African women. As Brown argues, "racialized patriarchy and sexualized concepts of race created new ways for white men to consolidate their power in a slave society."[20] Brown also suggests that as the colony developed formal legal systems and became ever more a slave society ruled by elite white men, white women's voices as arbiters of community opinion became more muted. While in the next chapter I will cover Brown's discussion of masculinity and "anxious patriarchs," this transformation to a revised patriarchal system suggests that not only racial distinctions but gender hierarchy among elites became more pronounced with the elaboration of slavery.

Gender was significant to the institution of slavery not only in Virginia (or in the US South more generally), but also in the Caribbean. As Hilary McD. Beckles has discussed, there were fewer African women than men brought from West Africa as slaves to the Caribbean. He attributes this to the dominant gender order in West Africa, where women worked in the fields and men were more dispensable and therefore likely to be sold into slavery. On West Indian plantations enslaved African men were forced to do what they would have considered women's work, that is, working in the fields. Although Englishmen did not expect white women to labor in the fields, because of the demand for workers, female indentured servants were imported from Britain from about 1624 to 1670. In the late seventeenth century English planters instituted a policy that no white women were to work in plantation labor gangs. To minimize the danger of interracial sex between white women and black men, they needed to be kept apart. As in the Virginia colony described by Brown, patriarchy became racialized. In the late seventeenth and early eighteenth centuries, planters became increasingly focused on enslaved African women's childbearing. Black women were expected both to bear children and to perform arduous labor. That they had a low birth rate was thought to indicate that they were unfeminine – they were cast as "Amazons." Plantation managers began offering financial incentives to slaves to reproduce in order to encourage the growth of the population of enslaved people (endangered by the abolition of the slave trade) and they encouraged young slaves to form Christian marriages to counter the claims of the abolitionists. Beckles argues, then, that African women were central to the institution of slavery and they were politically central to abolitionist and pro-slavery campaigns.[21]

Beckles' argument about the centrality of women's reproductive labor to slavery is supported and amplified by Jennifer Morgan in her book *Laboring Women: Reproduction and Gender in New World Slavery*. Morgan's work examines the significance of women and gender to seventeenth- and eighteenth-century slavery in the British Caribbean (Barbados) and the American South (South Carolina). By examining sixteenth- and seventeenth-century images and travelers' descriptions of African women, she argues that such representations show the emergence of notions of racialized difference that helped to legitimate the slave trade. Most significantly, African women were depicted as both physically strong and accustomed to giving birth in public and returning shortly thereafter to their productive labors. Although enslaved women did not give birth to many children, as Beckles had suggested, the descriptions of them in the British colonies focused on their capacity to both give birth and do manual labor, justifying their dual capacities as slaves to bring profit to their masters. African women were described as giving birth without pain, distinguishing them from European women. Using probate records and wills from late seventeenth- and eighteenth-century Barbados and South Carolina, Morgan shows that slave owners saw wealth accumulating through enslaved women's childbearing and thus they might will one young female slave to two separate heirs.[22]

These studies on the significance of gender to slavery and to the creation of racial distinctions suggest that sex and the body were of critical importance to New World slavery and in the creation of identities differentiated by "race." This crucial connection, about which we will have more to say later in discussions concerning colonial and imperial projects, has been explored in some detail by Kirsten Fischer in *Suspect Relations: Sex, Race, and Resistance in Colonial North Carolina*. Basing her research on lower court records in North Carolina in the eighteenth century, she illuminates how ordinary people in the colony contributed to the meaning of racial difference in cases dealing with violence (especially of a sexual nature) and interracial sexual slander. It was especially in cases of interracial sexual relationships that ordinary people articulated ideas about the significance of race. Fischer shows that during the eighteenth century white servants and black slaves were punished differently. Whereas in the seventeenth century servants might be branded or have their tongues or ears cut off, such punishments in the eighteenth century were meted out only to black slaves. In the mid-eighteenth century a law was passed in North Carolina prescribing castration for male slaves convicted of a first offense. Such a policy clearly links anxieties about sexuality and the hardening of racial distinctions. A law prohibiting interracial marriage was passed in the colony in 1715 and was made more stringent in mid-century legislation that extended the prohibition to persons with any traceable African heritage. As Fischer put it, "Unlawful sex was symbolically linked to ideas of racial difference in ways that made race seem as corporeal as sex."[23] White masters would escape punishment for sexually exploiting enslaved women, and African women would be publicly whipped while naked. The heads of African men accused of rape were displayed on roadside poles. Thus violence also had a sexual dimension, one that underscored the connection between gendered race and sex.

In the post-emancipation British Colony of the Cape, South Africa, "race," in combination with marital status, was critical in defining respectable womanhood. Pamela Scully's investigation of rape cases in the Colony after slavery ended in 1838 shows the "centrality of sexuality in the constitution of colonial identities," while revealing how colonial rule was shaped by "implicit assumptions about race, gender, and class."[24] She suggests that colonialism (as well as slavery) created conditions that shielded white men from punishment for raping black women. Scully's analysis of the dynamics of race, sex, and gender in the middle of the nineteenth century focuses on the case of a young black male laborer accused of raping the wife of a farmer. The man admitted his guilt and was sentenced to death for his crime. Upon receiving petitions in the laborer's defense put forward by *white* men claiming that the woman in question who brought the charge of rape was a woman of color, the man's death sentence was commuted, ostensibly because she was thought to have been wanton sexually. The farmer and his wife were both suspected of being of mixed heritage ("Bastard coloured persons") by people in the local community. The judge originally had believed the victim to have been a white woman and therefore did not question her respectability. This came into question, however, when she was believed to be "black." But why did white men petition on behalf of black men accused of rape? It turns out that this was not an isolated instance. Scully found other cases in which white men had taken up the cause of black men accused of rape. In all of these cases, the women who were the victims were perceived by the white community as being black. If a white woman was raped, the rapist's race determined the nature of his sentence. Scully hypothesizes that the white petitioners defended black men accused of raping a black woman as a way of denying that the rape of a black woman was a crime punishable by death (no matter who raped her) because black women were by nature sexually licentious beings without honor. This was a way, she suggests, for white men to retain sexual access to black women without putting themselves in legal jeopardy. Scully's analysis once again demonstrates the interdependence of gender and race and underscores the significance of sexuality, especially interracial sexual relations, for colonial rule – for distinguishing colonized and colonizer and demarcating difference.

Feminist scholars studying various colonial sites in different periods have revealed the centrality of racialized gender and intimate spaces for the processes of colonization and colonial rule. Anxieties about sexuality and marriage were preoccupations of colonial governance in Asia, Africa, North America, and the Caribbean. Such anxieties informed questions about the nature of social order and about how colonizers and rulers could be kept distinct from the colonized and ruled; thus were indelibly bound up with the politics of race. How they played out at different times and in different circumstances may not have been the same, but they were critical preoccupations in all imperial social formations.[25] Philippa Levine summarizes the significance of gender and sexuality to the British Empire, indicating that "[u]nrestrained sexuality was an unending threat to Empire; it undermined notions of British moderation and rationality, it produced interracial liaisons and sometimes offspring; it encouraged and facilitated unauthorized sexual behaviours considered dangerous or unseemly. These were not minor considerations but central to the functioning of imperial governance."[26]

Concubinage (non-marital cohabitation involving European men and indigenous women), prostitution, the exclusion and then importation of European women, the universal prohibition of sexual contact between white women and non-white men, fears about non-white men sexually assaulting white women, and the question of who could legally marry whom – all at various points were aspects of colonial governance in different imperial projects.

Ann Stoler has argued that concubinage, legal in the Dutch East Indies until the twentieth century, was actively tolerated in order to keep "men in their barracks and bungalows, out of brothels and less inclined to perverse liaisons with one another."[27] This practice, as well as the regulation of prostitution in India, as Philippa Levine has shown, was instituted on the assumption that men were, by nature, highly sexed and needed to be restrained so that the Empire would retain its image as a civilizing agent.[28] Native women, like the European women who were later brought to the colonies to form (marital) domestic relations with white men, were thought to keep men content and fit for work. Stoler maintains that concubinage was the preferred form of domestic relationship in the Dutch East Indies as long as the dominance of European men was secure, although the bases of that dominance might vary. Surveying research on a range of colonial settings, Stoler found that when European women did arrive, European versions of marital domesticity prevailed and concern with racial difference became increasingly pronounced. Mary Procida's study of the women in the Anglo-Indian community in British India suggests that white women were antagonistic toward Indian women and men, intent upon preserving their own and their husbands' privileged positions, and thus were not simply passive bystanders in the broader dynamics of colonial rule.[29] Stoler argues, however, that "[t]he voices of European women...had little resonance until their objections coincided with a realignment in racial and class politics."[30]

White British women were brought to British Columbia, Canada, in the 1860s immigration schemes by the colonial state to bring respectability, morality, and domesticity to the colony. Adele Perry's study of gender and race in the making of British Columbia indicates that their presence was meant to "serve as boundary markers between races" by eliminating mixed-race relationships and to bring respectability to the colony by domesticating and reforming Euro-Canadian men. Her analysis, however, shows that their presence was a "mixed blessing" for the colonial authorities. The exigencies of living there under conditions in which they were financially dependent and without opportunities for labor meant that they did not always conform to imperial visions of white womanhood.

In the outposts of the British Empire of western Canada from the late seventeenth century to the last decades of the eighteenth century, fur traders and native women married, as Sylvia Van Kirk's 1981 study showed. No white women were present in this part of Canada until the early nineteenth century. But domesticity was important to the fur traders, and the aboriginal community encouraged unions between their women and the male traders to enhance economic ties by incorporating Euro-Canadian men into kinship networks. Thus, intermarriage and the development of kinship ties were of fundamental importance to the development of the fur trade. The form of marriage that was enacted drew upon both Indian and European customs and was known as marriage *à la façon du pays*, after the custom of the country. But in the period of settlement, such marriages became increasingly rare and were denigrated by white society. As a consequence the sexual exploitation of native women increased and marriage *à la façon du pays* was considered illegal and immoral. Van Kirk emphasizes that the marriages that had taken place between white fur traders and native women led to what she called "many tender ties" – feelings of deep affection between Indian women and their Euro-Canadian husbands that developed and endured.[32]

In a recent essay Van Kirk argues that by the late nineteenth century, when intermarriage between aboriginal women and Euro-Canadian men occurred, the women lost their legal status as Indians, in contrast to the earlier period, when marriage was customarily seen as a way of integrating Euro-Canadian men into networks of Indian kin. She further suggests that while marriage between an aboriginal woman and a Euro-Canadian man might have been tolerated within colonial communities, there were very few examples of an aboriginal man marrying a Euro-Canadian woman. In the two cases that she presents where such marriages took place, they were met with pronounced hostility that she suggests stemmed from the threat of such relationships to Euro-Canadian male prerogatives. As settler society moved west over the course of the nineteenth century, intermarriage became increasingly denigrated and a racist rhetoric flourished, especially condemning what had come to be known as "miscegenation," or the mixing of "races." The children of such unions were thought to be degenerate.[33]

As research on Canada suggests, ideas about and attitudes toward "mixed" unions between colonizers and colonized differed over time and depending upon circumstances. Latin American scholars have pointed out that being of "mixed" heritage was valorized as a way of "whitening" the population to differentiate the indigenous population from those whose backgrounds were at least partially European. In British India, mixed unions were denigrated and policed. In the Dutch East Indies, mixed intimate relationships were at some points and for some colonial men encouraged and at other times condemned. In French Indochina and the Dutch East Indies, as well as in imperial governments in Europe, how to deal with and classify the offspring of those relationships was a persistent subject of concern and debate. In spite of these variations, gender and "race" were always categories at the very center of how the boundaries between colonized and colonizer could be drawn.[34]

Anxieties about intimate relationships between colonized and colonizer, European and "other," also could flourish in European metropoles. Tyler Stovall's research on an episode in France during World War I shows how profound fears about miscegenation circulated when a large number of colonized African men from Madagascar were brought to France to work in factories alongside the large number of French women who were also employed in heavy industry at the time to offset the wartime shortfall in labor. French authorities vigorously attempted to limit any possibilities of intimacy with French women in order to preserve gender and racial hierarchies both at home and in the empire. While the French welcomed Africans as soldiers because they were considered to be "savages," they also saw them as morally weak and sexually lustful, so their presence as workers was suspect. Working women in France, meanwhile, were denigrated because they were thought to be lazy and sexually immoral, and, like all women, to be emotionally out of control. From 1914, as France tried to recruit white spouses for French settlers in the colonies, women colonizers were imagined to exemplify bourgeois values of domesticity and gentility and in the colony they lived privileged lives. Thus, one issue that concerned the government was that sexual contact between French women workers and Africans would threaten the image of "*la coloniale*" both in the metropole and in Africa. The government also was deeply concerned by censors' reports that pornographic postcards were sent home by colonials. Stovall argues that "the prospect of nonwhite men looking at erotic French postcards inverted the colonial pattern of European men admiring salacious images of native women."[35] The authorities intervened in various ways to prevent interracial intimacy, including attempting to stop French women from marrying non-white men. These efforts were relatively unsuccessful, but Stovall suggests that they did help to establish "the very idea of a color line in France, particularly one governing relations between members of the opposite sex."[36]

Conclusion

This chapter has been concerned with demonstrating the ways that gender, race, and class need to be considered as overlapping and intersecting categories and relations. Examples of scholarship on philanthropic, missionary, and other beneficent activities have revealed how race/ethnicity and/or class combined with gender to shape ideas and practices. Research on slavery in North America and the Caribbean has shown the centrality of gender, reproduction, and the body to the creation and maintenance of New World slavery and to the construction of difference. Finally, placing gender at the center of scholarship on colonialism has shown how various forms of sexual intimacy between colonizers and the colonized were at the very heart of imperial projects because they put at risk the boundaries of rule. The next chapter considers how using gender as a tool of analysis is critical to understanding not only the changing meanings of womanhood, but has fostered the study of masculinities as a topic of gender history.

4
Men and Masculinity

A significant strand of feminist-inspired gender history has concerned men as gendered historical subjects and/or has explored the changing meanings of masculinity or manliness. An historical focus on men as men and on the meanings of masculinity is an especially significant contribution of gender history because professional history writing for so long had concerned itself with the political, social, and economic activities of men without recognizing them as gendered beings. That is, the historical actors in the narratives of history have been understood to be genderless. Those who were depicted as the agents of history were thought of as disembodied. Only women were understood to be embodied – as, for example, in the nineteenth century, when they were known as "the sex." The particularity of those who made history was overlooked or taken as "natural" in histories of nation building, war, industrialization, empire, and so forth. The idea that gender may have influenced the social actors, processes, and events involved in these histories was unexamined. As Michael S. Kimmel has emphasized, those who are in power or who are in elevated social positions are invisible to themselves "as specifically constituted groups."[1] They see themselves as "normal," as the unmarked universal, in spite of their relative social standing, while it is "those others" who are "different."

The development of gender history has encouraged historians to ask critical questions concerning how "maleness" and codes or norms of masculinity have been understood in the past and may have influenced the lives of both women and men. They aim to expose the activities of men as men to historical analysis and to analyze whether and how the diverse meanings of manliness, masculinity, or manhood have been implicated in a variety of kinds of regimes of power.

In this chapter I will use the terms "masculinity," "manliness," and "manhood" to refer to the gender norms and expectations, ideals and traits associated with being male. The term "masculinity," however, was not always used in the past and, in fact, the uses of the term have different histories depending upon the language being spoken. Throughout the nineteenth century in American English, the term "masculine" was used to "differentiate between things pertaining to men versus women"[2] – for example, "masculine clothing" as opposed to feminine attire. But it was in the twentieth century that the term "masculinity" came into use, and then, as we shall see, it had very specific meanings that differed from how manhood was understood earlier. The English term "masculinity" is derived from the French term "*masculinité*," a word that could be found in French dictionaries from at least the mid-eighteenth century. Historically, however, the masculine most often referred to language. The French were more likely to speak of traits like *virile* or *virilité*, which from the seventeenth century they understood in opposition to the effeminate.[3]

In writing histories of men as gendered social actors, scholars have investigated both how the social construction and experience of being male have influenced men's identities and their activities, and how these have differed across cultures and groups as well as over time. Importantly, scholars refer not to "masculinity," singular, but to "masculinities," plural, because they insist that there has never been just one way to "be a man"; rather, at any one time there may be several. What it has meant to be manly or masculine in a particular historical period varies depending upon other forms of difference and also upon the particular social contexts in which men are engaged. At any given point in time, men participate in various institutional settings, most importantly the family, the workplace, and all-male associations, as well as being involved in different kinds of associations at different points in their lives, such as school, the military, and the street corner.[4]

In any particular historical period, some meanings of manhood may become dominant. Influenced by the sociologist Raewyn Connell, historians have used the term "hegemonic" in referring to these dominant cultural constructions because it suggests not only the preeminence of a particular code of masculine attributes, but also that these ways of being a man are contested. But critically, the ones that are dominant or hegemonic seem "natural." They appear permanent – this is "how men are" or how "real men should be" – although they are, in fact, "contingent, fluid, socially and historically constructed, changeable and constantly changing."[5] These changes in the meanings of manliness, the coupling of potentially contradictory traits that men are supposed to exhibit at a single point in time, and the fact that there may be alternative versions of ideal manhood that coexist suggest that masculinity is an unstable gender formation.

Gender historians assume that manhood and womanhood are defined in relation to one another. Furthermore, they acknowledge that the relationships between men and women have been unequal ones – characterized by differential power. Yet to be manly or masculine historically has not simply been seen in opposition to "femaleness." John Tosh has argued that "manliness" in nineteenth-century Britain was only "secondarily about relations with women." It was, rather, about the "inner character of man, and with the kind of behaviour which displayed this character in the world at large."[6] Stefan Dudink has pointed out that in early modern Holland, "masculinity was defined not so much in terms of a given difference from femininity, as in terms of a dangerous proximity to effeminacy."[7] In other words, to be "manly" was the opposite of being "unmanly" or effeminate. Such an understanding of manliness or masculinity suggests that manhood is as much concerned with relationships among men as it is about a gender hierarchy in which men have power over women. In addition, anthropologist David Gilmore has argued that in most societies manhood must be demonstrated – it is a status that must be tested and proved.[8] Manliness or masculinity "is always subject to scrutiny, lapses, and failed performances, and is thus forever in a contested state."[9] These are themes that will recur in the historical research discussed in this chapter.

In her study of how boys became men in late medieval Europe, Ruth Mazo Karras has shown that while definitions of manhood may have presumed that manhood was antithetical to womanliness, manliness was about boys becoming men by dominating or successfully competing against other men. Most medieval men, she suggests, took women's subordinate place in society for granted, and the subjection of women was "always a part of masculinity, but not always its purpose or its central feature."[10] Karras focused her analysis on three groupings of men – knights, university students, and urban craftsmen – in the period between about 1300 and 1500. Although knights might claim that they were jousting to win the love of a woman, their fighting prowess was meant to impress other men as it was these other men who evaluated the young knight and would confirm his aristocratic manhood. The main measure of manhood was the successful demonstration of violence in the field of battle. The medieval university was another realm in which young men acquired manhood through competition. There they engaged in intellectual battles using their "intellect to dominate other men."[11] Masculinity was confirmed in initiation rituals through which men bonded with one another while women were viewed as sexual objects. For university students, masculinity was associated with moderation and rationality, characteristics that distinguished them not only from women, but also from beasts.

In the urban craft workshop, to become a man meant "proving oneself not a boy."[12] A young man was meant to be learning how to master his craft, to prove himself not a woman or a child by having a skill and achieving independence, thus demonstrating that he was capable of being "a substantial citizen." Women were tangential to different medieval masculinities, but that was largely because at the time their subordination was taken for granted. They primarily mattered to the demonstration of manliness only insofar as they served in one way or another to validate men's superiority in the eyes of other men.

In a sophisticated analysis of manhood in early modern England, primarily in the period between the mid-sixteenth and mid-seventeenth centuries, Alexandra Shepard analyzes both how normative patriarchal manhood was defined in prescriptive literature and medical texts and the ways that men engaged in the social practices of manhood. Manhood was frequently referred to at the time as an "estate," suggesting it was a status with associated privileges. While manhood was based on gender difference, the estate of manhood was linked to being an adult male – a phase in the life cycle – associated with being a married head of household. Thus age, marital status, and increasingly social status were routes to attaining patriarchal manhood and its concomitant privileges. Men who attained manhood were thought to have the sort of bearing or persona that enabled them to govern their own passions as well as the behavior of dependants and those of lower rank. Manhood had other attributes as well, including honesty and thrift, strength and authority, moderation, reason, and wit – qualities invoked at different times and in different circumstances; qualities that also were subject to different interpretations. Importantly, Shepard argues that while patriarchal manhood may have been defined in relation to women, not all men could achieve it, and "manhood was often most resonantly worked out between men."[13]

Not all men could achieve full economic independence. Those who were young and poor, especially, found alternative ways of asserting their manhood. Young men, for example, "subverted patriarchal concepts of manhood rooted in thrift, order, and self-control through rituals of excess."[14] They established their manhood "primarily amongst their peers, and often in opposition to their elders."[15] They might engage in "nightwalking," drinking to excess, acts of vandalism or violence, and the pursuit of illicit sex, celebrating "counter-codes of manhood rooted in prodigality, transience, violence, bravado, and debauchery."[16] While such behavior on the part of Cambridge University students was frequently condemned, local authorities often tacitly approved of their youthful manly displays, overlooking their misdeeds. Working men also might enact other forms of manliness, as, for example, at the alehouse or tavern, where camaraderie with other men, not to mention drinking large quantities of alcohol, was a central feature.

Shepard devotes considerable attention to the significance of violence for manhood, and she suggests that the deployment of violence made for contradictions within patriarchal manliness. While violence was used to enforce patriarchal norms, it also was appropriated by men who were excluded from positions of authority. It was a primary way in which men disciplined subordinates, challenged authority, or defended their reputations. Shepard's work shows not only that manhood was often defined relative to and constructed in the company of other men, but also provides an example of how alternative forms of manliness challenged hegemonic masculinity, making it an unstable formation.

Chapter 3 discussed the complex interdependence of race and gender affecting white and enslaved women in the early English colony of Virginia studied by Kathleen Brown. Brown also underscores the instability of hegemonic, patriarchal manhood in the Virginia colony.[17] As both Shepard and Brown suggest, English patriarchal manhood and the political authority based upon it were predicated on attaining the status of an independent householder. But in the colony there was a shortage of English women, and many of the men who had come to Virginia as colonizers had to endure long periods of service in the employ of others. Married property owners in the frontier areas were under continual pressure to defend themselves from Indians, whose lands they occupied. They also resented the wealthy leaders of the colony, especially the colony's governor, William Berkeley, who was accused of political favoritism and of failing to support them in their struggles against incursions by Indians. Elite men in some of the oldest counties of the colony were being challenged by "outspoken women, religious dissidents, unruly servants and slaves," threatening their domestic and political authority.[18]

These sources of unease fueled a leadership crisis that in turn led to a major rebellion in 1676. Brown understands Bacon's Rebellion as a conflict between "two distinct cultures of masculinity."[19] On the one side elite planters expressed their political position in terms of male honor – central to both their manhood and their class status. On the other were the small planters, the powerless white male householders who attempted to establish their manhood through the barrel of a gun in order to defend themselves and their property from Indians. They also demanded that the Colony's leadership support their efforts against the Indians and claimed the right to resist what they experienced as unjust treatment from the elite in authority. Their leader was Nathaniel Bacon, whose name became associated with the rebellion. Servants and slaves joined in to further destabilize the transplanted patriarchal order.

The rebellion ended with Bacon's death and the arrival of royal commissioners sent by the King to investigate the conflict. In the post-rebellion years, a political settlement was eventually reached with the passage of laws that had as their effect a new cross-class white Anglo-Virginian masculinity that defined itself against both African and Indian masculinity as well as against women. It revitalized patriarchal social forms, bolstering the domestic authority of ordinary men, and helped to forge an "authentic Anglo-Virginian identity" for elite men.[20]

In a concluding chapter of her book, Brown suggests that in the first half of the eighteenth century Virginia's elite planters had become more secure than their counterparts had been in the seventeenth century. Importantly, however, she insists that they continued to be apprehensive about the legitimacy and stability of their status. For Colonial gentlemen, authority was a "delicate project." It was especially their domestic authority that was under constant challenge. Slaves escaped, children rebelled, and wives resisted their husband's will. An orderly and genteel society in Virginia based upon an ideal of domestic tranquillity was never secure, especially as it was founded upon the violence of slavery. And as we learned from Shepard's analysis, violence and reactions to it had the potential to undermine patriarchal authority as well as to confront the planters with the fact, as Brown maintains, "that much of their authority depended upon their ability to inflict pain."[21]

Anne Lombard's research has investigated what it meant to "grow up male" in the period from the late seventeenth century through the eighteenth century in Colonial New England. Puritan "middling people," such as shopkeepers and craftsmen, migrated to the Massachusetts Bay Colony in the mid-sixteenth century. Like their counterparts in the

English metropole during this period, manhood for them meant economic independence. Property owning and/or self-employment was the prerequisite for independence, or what in the colony was termed "competence." Manly attributes, Lombard argues, had to be acquired, and claims to manhood were based on a man demonstrating that he had attained "rationality, self-control and mastery over whatever was passionate, sensual, and natural in the male self."[22] Manhood was defined partly in contrast to femininity, but importantly, it was also defined in comparison with boyhood or dependence. Someone who was an independent head of household and responsible for a family was more likely to be considered manly.

Puritanism was absolutely central to the inhabitants of the Colony. It promulgated a hierarchical society in which fathers ruled because they were believed able to rationally govern both their households and the polity, controlling "a passionate, uncontrolled, and sensual majority of dependent women, youths, children, servants and enslaved Africans."[23] Puritans believed that boys had to be prevented from dependence on their mothers and indulging in childish feelings, and thus fathers played an active role in rearing their sons, training them for their eventual status as independent men. Both peer relationships and romantic love were suspect, and it was only by learning "self-mastery, rationality, and control over the passions" that a youth could develop the qualities he needed to become a man.[24]

As in early modern England and in the Virginia Colony, and in spite of the emphasis on self-discipline and self-control in definitions of manhood, physical force and violence were associated with manhood in the seventeenth- and eighteenth-century New England colonies. Fathers could use force to discipline children, wives, and youth and also against other men who threatened their property. But Lombard's assessment of court cases suggests that patterns of violence changed in the early to mid-eighteenth century. There was a decline in violent conflicts over property, but a rise in the occurrence of fights between "gentlemen" and laborers. Fights increasingly erupted around taverns. In addition, there was an increase in disruptive behavior by youths that could involve attacks against householders. The resort to violence to maintain or threaten manly honor unsettled Puritan manhood, based as it was on rational self-control and patriarchal authority.

The studies of Anglo-American manhood in the early modern period discussed above suggest that the violent confrontations between men, especially the use of violence by patriarchs against subordinates, beset patriarchal manhood with contradictions. Violent confrontations involving duels between men of the *same* social standing, however, had a long life as an accepted means of settling disputes in France, as Robert Nye's research has shown. Nye argues that this was part of a medieval code of honor shaped by the values of noble warriors that persisted through the nineteenth century and was adopted by middle-class men even as what it meant to be a man changed dramatically. He suggests that such honor codes regulated men's relationships in professional life, sport, and politics. The duel was a highly rule-bound and orderly way that men publicly defended their honor and settled disputes which erupted between them. By participating in a duel, a man visibly demonstrated his physical heroism and courage, which was essential for his honor required constant reaffirmation. Ironically, the duel, once associated with the nobility, "helped promote equality because no man could refuse to cross swords with a legitimate opponent at the risk of personal shame and public ridicule."[25]

A second source of honor was linked to male heterosexuality. Nye focuses in particular on a variety of medical and political discourses that show in different ways that a man's identity was rooted in the sex of his body and that his sexual capacity and practice were continuing issues of public concern. As Nye states, for nineteenth-century French middle-class men, "a man's honor was now embedded deep in the blood and bones of his sex."[26] He suggests that because dishonor was seen to be related to sexual disorder, a man was compelled to maintain his honor. Therefore, the duel was a primary testing ground of bourgeois manhood – but it was a ground on which "a man was in greatest danger of dishonoring himself at the very moment he most expressly affirmed his honor."[27]

Nye's discussion of the scientific discourses concerning the male body suggests that there was growing anxiety about men's sexual energy in the last decades of the nineteenth century and the years leading up to World War I. This anxiety was associated with a host of others following the Franco-Prussian War, including the falling birth rate, fears of national decline, and apprehensions about sexual degeneracy. The medical texts that Nye examined indicated that while women's sexuality was taken for granted, men's sexuality was seen as problematic. The poor sexual health of the male body, understood to be especially threatened by intellectual pursuits, was believed to be responsible for the declining vitality of the French nation. The end of the nineteenth century in France witnessed what a number of scholars have termed a "crisis of masculinity."

This theme is explored by Christopher E. Forth, who focuses on the Dreyfus Affair, a political scandal that preoccupied France in the late nineteenth and early twentieth centuries. Alfred Dreyfus, a Jewish military captain, was falsely accused and convicted of treason in 1894 for giving military secrets to the Germans. Dreyfus was publicly condemned and humiliated. He protested his innocence, but in his retrial in 1899 military officials and the French intelligence service covered over evidence that someone else had committed the crime, enraging his supporters. Both his supporters and his detractors mobilized images of manhood in their vituperative debate. Their common ground, Forth argues, was their shared anxiety about the state of French manhood. At stake were two versions of manhood: a traditional, elite manliness associated with action and adventure and one associated with intellectuals and men whose livelihoods depended on mental rather than physical labor. Anti-Semitism was a key feature of the affair, in part because of the long-standing belief that Jewish men were weak and cowardly, bookish and effeminate. In the ensuing debate about Dreyfus, which continued until he was exonerated in 1906, those convinced of his guilt, even if they denounced anti-Semitism, focused on his cowardice and lack of honor. Dreyfus's defenders asserted that they were resolutely manly because they courageously promoted the truth. They attacked his accusers for being weak and unable to control themselves – suggesting the accusers were effeminate. Jewish men supporting the innocence of Dreyfus and opposing the miscarriage of justice that had imprisoned and exiled him "insisted upon their patriotism and martial prowess and downplayed their reputation for bookishness and physical weakness."[28] They allied themselves with ancient Hebrew soldiers, thus celebrating a martial ideal of manliness. And increasingly in the 1890s a muscular conception of masculinity became predominant in France, undermining the efforts of the pro-Dreyfus supporters to insist on the manliness of intellectual men. True masculinity "proved its virility through deeds that required force rather than simple assertions of physical vitality."[29] Forth argues that it was this "culture of force" associated with physical fitness and training that influenced the generation of men who were to fight in World War I. Thus, what some might argue was a "crisis of masculinity" in France was eventually resolved, at least for a time, as an aggressive and muscular code of manliness became the celebrated ideal.

Forth notes in the conclusion to his book that the "crisis of French manhood" as it expressed itself in the Dreyfus Affair was occurring elsewhere in the Western world at about the same time. Across both Europe and North America, as Angus McLaren has shown, anxiety about the nature of manhood was widespread – manhood was "under siege" at the turn of the twentieth century, and masculinity was "going through a period of deconstruction and reconstruction."[30] Many of the social ills of the time were blamed on a failure of manliness: the declining birth rate, the physical weakness of working-class urban youth in Britain, who were rejected as recruits for the armed services, weakening industrial strength, labor unrest, juvenile crime, and so forth. In the United States, physicians discovered a new disease, "neurasthenia," that threatened to afflict professional and business men because they did mental rather than physical labor. There and elsewhere medical doctors and others became ever more concerned about homosexuality, which they saw as a threatening malady and degenerate identity. The muscular, aggressive, and vigorously heterosexual man became the dominant masculine ideal, underscored by scientists, doctors, judges, and journalists in various countries.

In the United States, as Gail Bederman has argued, middle-class men became "unusually obsessed" with manhood during this period. She attributes this to a variety of challenges that they faced that affected their sense of what it meant to be a man. Manliness in the nineteenth century had emphasized self-control, moral strength, and a powerful will. Strength was thought to stem from self-restraint and mastery over the passions. Economic independence and being head of a household were primary goals. Threats to men's ability to live up to these ideals stemmed from increasing economic insecurity, decreasing opportunities for self-employment, and narrowing career prospects. Men also felt threatened on a number of other fronts: the middle-class women's movement challenged men's monopoly of politics as well as the professions; the growth of consumerism and new leisure pursuits tested the ethos of self-denial and hard work with one emphasizing pleasure and fun; and labor unrest and immigration unsettled middle-class men's sense of place. In response they transformed their notions of ideal manhood from those characterizing what had been "manliness" to "masculinity." Bederman suggests that there were various ways that different men attempted to remake manhood, including joining fraternal orders, celebrating muscular sports, and fostering the spread of organizations such as the Boy Scouts. In countering the perceived threats to their manhood through such a variety of activities, understandings of the nature of white, middle-class American manhood changed from those associated with manliness to masculinity, which encompassed traits such as aggressiveness, physical force, and "virile" heterosexuality.

Central to the remaking of American manhood was a notion of civilization and its relationship to race. Civilization was understood as a stage in evolution that legitimated and explained white, male dominance. The discourse of civilization was fluid and could be used to justify various claims to power, but it was especially white middle-class and more elite men who claimed it to legitimate their rule. At the same time they associated themselves with a more "primitive ethos" that celebrated their virility. Theodore Roosevelt exemplified the ideal type of a man who embodied both tendencies. "Combining manliness and masculinity, civilization and the primitive, Roosevelt modeled a new type of manhood for the American people.... Through this new type of manhood, Roosevelt claimed not only a personal power for himself but also a collective imperialistic manhood for the white American race."[31]

Was America's "obsession" with manhood at the end of the nineteenth and beginning of the twentieth century a "crisis"? Bederman argues, "no." Rather, what she calls "ideologies of gender" are always contested and beset with contradictions and therefore are unstable. Michael Kimmel argues similarly that masculinity "is unresolved – never able to be fully demonstrated, subject to eternal doubt. Masculinity needs constant validation; its pursuit is relentless."[32] Feminist scholar Lynne Segal suggests that "masculinity has always been crisis-ridden."[33] Possibly because men and the traits attributed to them (in contrast to women) have been so closely associated with power, social, economic, and political changes that are seen to unsettle relationships of power arouse widespread concern about the nature of manhood. Ironically, then, power or dominance, because it is never total, makes the meanings or ideologies of manhood inherently unstable. But it is only at particular historical moments when that instability surfaces to produce significant historical effects.

The mid-nineteenth century in the United States was one such time, as Amy Greenberg's research suggests. Economic transformations made men's livelihoods and occupational opportunities less certain than they had been. The suffrage movement challenged the gender order politically. "For men the experience of work and home life, of social interactions, even of citizenship was dramatically transformed from the 1830s to 1859s."[34] These unsettling changes led to competition for cultural dominance or hegemony between the ideals of "martial" and "restrained" manhood. Those who espoused the values of "restrained manhood" saw manliness as grounded in "being morally upright, reliable, and brave."[35] They disdained violent sports and drinking to excess, and placed household and family at the center of their lives, supporting women's domesticity. Martial manhood, by contrast, valued strength and physical aggression and the ability to dominate both women and other men. These different masculinities cut across class distinctions and all who espoused them believed in America's Manifest Destiny, although they dramatically differed in what that was to entail. The term

"Manifest Destiny," coined in 1845, referred to America's conquest of the West, to foreign expansion (such as America's acquisition of the Southwest from Texas to California as a result of winning its war with Mexico), and more generally to the eventual rise of America's global influence. Those Americans (both men and women) who supported a martial masculinity advocated that the United States extend its territory through force. Those favoring restrained manhood argued that America's Manifest Destiny should be achieved through commerce and trade and through proselytizing its presumed superior social, political, and religious forms abroad rather than by aggressive territorial expansionism. Using a variety of documents, including letters, newspapers, travel accounts, and diaries, Greenberg shows that debates over Manifest Destiny were disputes over gender meanings and that martial men both supported and engaged in filibustering – going into foreign countries (including Cuba, Nicaragua, and Mexico) to instigate or incite insurrections. Many of the men who joined these unsuccessful adventures were those who were economic failures at home, but their exploits and the causes that were said to justify them were applauded by men who shared a vision of the triumph of American martial manhood. In the 1850s aggressive expansionism and the ideal of martial manhood dominated debates over America's role in the world. Greenberg argues that this gendered culture "encouraged Northerners and Southerners to turn to violence as a solution to personal and national problems," and "helped turn sectional differences into cause for [civil] war."[36]

Although, according to Greenberg, restrained masculinity became the preferred masculine ideal following the American Civil War, which ended in 1865, we learned from Gail Bederman's research discussed above that around the turn of the century anxieties about manhood were again aroused due to a host of political, social, and economic changes that especially affected middle- and upper-class men. Kristin L. Hoganson argues that these men, in particular, "feared that a decline in manly character would impair their ability to maintain not only their class, racial and national privileges, but also their status relative to women," especially given the gender politics of the suffrage movement and the rise of what became known then as the "assertive New Women," who "scoffed at the submissive ideals of womanhood."[37] Based on her examination of the public rhetoric about US foreign policy and the debates leading to the Spanish–American and the Philippine–American wars, Hoganson convincingly argues that these anxieties about manliness "helped push the nation into war by fostering a desire for martial challenges."[38] Participants in the debate who espoused a bellicose attitude, called "jingoes" at the time, used gendered imagery to depict the fate of Cuba in Spanish hands, and argued that intervening in Cuba's independence struggle from Spain would give American men the opportunity to assume their manly duty to "bolster chivalry and honor in the United States." In debates about whether to once again fight the Spanish, this time over the Philippines, imperialists portrayed themselves as "virile young men," and anti-imperialists as "carping old women." Those on the opposite side in these debates also attempted to present themselves as manly, but they emphasized their "supposed maturity, self-restraint and resemblance to the nation's fathers."[39] They argued that the militarists would "subvert manly freedom of opinion," turning American men into "civic cowards."[40] It was not, therefore, all men who adopted a war-like stance. But all the participants in the debate called upon one or the other form of manhood in arguing the merits of their position. Hoganson does not argue that ideas about manhood caused these wars. Rather, her work supports the point that because a convergence of social, political, and economic factors aroused anxieties about manhood in late nineteenth-century America, these concerns stimulated and were particularly pronounced in the debate about war and empire that took place at this time.

The interconnections of masculinity with relations of power are, perhaps, nowhere more clearly at play than in the politics of British colonialism in India. Mrinalini Sinha's important analysis of the "practices of ruling" in British India illuminates how the stereotypical figures of the "manly Englishman" and the "effeminate Bengali" were constituted and became the rhetorical grounds upon which colonial rulers and native elites engaged with one another in the late nineteenth century.[41] She argues that the ideology of colonial masculinity developed within what she calls an "imperial social formation" that included both Britain and India. Thus, the "manly Englishman" was a figure that arose in the late nineteenth century in the context of anxieties about manhood within the British metropole, given the perceived threat of feminism along with a confluence of economic and political unease, and in India, as a result of concerns about and the demands of elite Bengali men for a greater "share in the exclusive privileges of the British colonial elite."[42] Sinha shows that when, in 1883–4, a bill was proposed to allow Indian men to try British men in colonial courts, the Anglo-Indian press deployed the image of the "effeminate Babu," who was presumed unfit to assume such manly duties. Thus, gender difference was substituted for racial difference as the grounds upon which Anglo-Indians attempted to reassert their imperial interests. Interestingly, Anglo-Indian women actively joined the opposition against the bill, making some Anglo-Indian men concerned that women's political partici-pation would unsettle the gender order of Anglo-Indian society. The opposition of Anglo-Indian men to the bill not only likened the "unfitness of native civilians to the unfitness of women" to take on responsible public positions. It claimed that natives were by nature timid men devoid of both "manly physique" and "manly character," and thus they were "unfit to exercise authority over the 'manly Englishman' or even over the other manly native races of India."[43]

Although the idea that some men made better soldiers than others because they were more "martial" had existed in one form or another for some time, work by Heather Streets argues that it was the Indian Rebellion of 1857 that was a crucial event in the construction of the idea of martial races.[44] The Rebellion was framed as an attack by "unmanly Hindu cowards" against British women and children. The troops defending British rule became associated with the opposite characteristics. The Sikhs from the Punjab, the Highlanders from Scotland, and the Gurkhas from Nepal were constructed as "fierce, gallant, honourable and courageous" in light of their actions during the Rebellion. In later years British mili-tary officers saw them as exemplars of military masculinity as they "felt themselves challenged on all sides by the simul-taneous spectres of Russian expansion into India's northwest frontier region, German militarism, British recruiting difficul-ties, and Indian and Irish nationalism."[45] While Russian expansion and German militarism were perceived as threats from without to British imperial manhood, feminist campaigns against licensed prostitution in India and the upsurge of Indian and Irish nationalism were experienced as challenges from within the Empire. Streets suggests that the language of martial race masculinity was a "strategy of domination and rule that used the power and appeal of racial and gendered language for political purposes."[46] During the Second Afghan War of 1878–80, Commanding Officer Frederick Roberts used the British press to advertise his military feats and deflect criticism, and depicted the extreme difficulties facing the army in the northwest frontier, which required participation of Highlanders, Sikhs, and Gurkhas, who were reputed to display "physical prowess, unrestrained bravery and solidarity of spirit to defend the Empire."[47] His reports and the commentaries in the press about the successes of his troops furthered the belief that certain "races" of men were especially "manly men." It was due, in part, to his accounts that the connection between and reputation of the "Highlanders and South Asian 'martial races' originally made during the Rebellion" and again during the Afghan War became part of British popular culture.[48]

Streets argues that martial race discourse was beset by the "very anxieties which had produced it in the first place.... Worries over whether the 'martial races' would themselves some day degenerate, or whether these 'races' would in fact really be able to stand up to a European enemy, crept into military writings as quickly as martial race discourse attempted to ease them with its seamless narratives of confidence."[49] Thus even the masculinity supposedly exemplified by those thought to be men of the "martial races" was haunted by the potential of civilization to emasculate them – a fear that appears to have grown stronger toward the end of the nineteenth century and in the first years of the twentieth.

Both Streets' research on martial race ideology in Britain and Gail Bederman's analysis of the interconnections of race, masculinity, and civilization in the early twentieth-century United States suggest the ambivalent lure of the "primitive" in this period. In the United States, according to Bederman, white men declared their superiority over African American men by claiming for themselves the traits associated with "primitive" men – muscularity, physical strength, and an aggressive spirit. After the black prize fighter Jack Johnson fought and won the heavyweight championship from the white boxer Tommy Burns in 1908, whites across the United States clamored for a former retired white champion boxer, Jim Jeffries, to reenter the ring and seize the title. Jeffries agreed, as he said, "for the sole purpose of proving that a white man is better than a negro."[50] The fight that took place in Reno, Nevada, in 1910 was won by Johnson in a "bloody rout," and, as Bederman has written, "the defenders of white male supremacy were very publicly hoist by their own petards."[51] Riots broke out across the country as whites went on the rampage expressing their fury against black men who were celebrating the Johnson victory. A few weeks later the US Congress passed a law suppressing fight films. Eventually the national Bureau of Investigation was ordered to find something to discredit Johnson, which they succeeded in doing, and, to avoid prison, Johnson left the country.

Race, manhood, and boxing also were issues elsewhere in the world, as Patrick McDevitt has shown.[52] The fight in which Johnson had initially won the world championship took place in Sydney, Australia, and Tommy Burns, his opponent, was a white Canadian. The fight attracted significant interest in Australia, where the pre-fight press coverage began at least six months in advance and focused heavily on the relative merits of white and black manhood. Tens of thousands paid to see the fight or tried to get tickets for it, and around 7,000 people queued to see films of the bout two days afterward.[53] Not surprisingly, then, the public in Britain and the Commonwealth eagerly anticipated the fight between Jeffries and Johnson.

In the aftermath of the boxing match, the British House of Commons discussed but did not act on the issue of banning fight films, though the government of South Africa, where the issue of race was more fractious, prevented movies of the contest from being shown. When Johnson arranged to fight a favorite English boxer in Britain, however, a campaign to ban the bout ensued. Opposition to the match came from various sources, but it was its opponents in the Home Office who won the day. Although one object was to keep the peace, McDevitt quotes official government documents indicating that it was primarily "to prevent a meeting in the Prize Ring of a black and a white man in the Capital of the Empire."[54] The case formed a precedent that prevented any major match between white and non-white boxers into the 1930s in the United Kingdom. McDevitt argues that the underlying motive for the ban was that if a black man were to win such a match, it would "erode the mythology of British superiority at home and abroad."[55] Underlying this was anxiety that "civilization" which supposedly made the British "superior" both at home and abroad had degenerating effects on British men. During the period, however, boxing grew ever more popular as a "display of muscular male bodies enduring pain and physically dominating other men," fed, as McDevitt argues, on "white male fears of black men and national degeneration."[56]

Thus far this chapter has been concerned with examples of gender historians' analyses of the discourses or ideologies of manhood in the context of men's relations with one another. But what of men's lives at home, in their households and with their families? Leonore Davidoff and Catherine Hall's ground-breaking study of gender and the making of the middle class in the late eighteenth and first half of the nineteenth centuries in England, *Family Fortunes*, demonstrates the centrality of marriage and fatherhood in men's lives. Under the influence of evangelicalism, domesticity was the basis of a moral and religious life for both men and women. Family and household were the foundations of business enterprises, and the aim of the business establishment was the survival and well-being of the family.[57] Men retired from business or professional life as early as possible to devote themselves to a variety of civic and religious activities, but most especially to their homes and gardens. The myriad local sources investigated by the authors reveal men's intense involvement with their families and their "loving interest" in their children's lives.[58] Their evidence clearly demonstrated that into old age uncles, fathers, and grandfathers played with the many children who might be around the house and yard, and fathers were gravely concerned with their children's illnesses. "Fatherhood was a responsibility and an enjoyment...part of a moral destiny."[59]

Building upon *Family Fortunes*, and drawing on etiquette manuals as well as private diaries and letters, John Tosh's analysis of middle-class men's lives in Victorian England probes the significance of domesticity for masculinity from the 1830s through the turn of the next century. By domesticity he intends to denote not simply a type of residence or set of obligations, but "a profound attachment: a state of mind as well as a physical orientation."[60] Masculine domesticity was exalted from the 1830s to the 1860s. These were the years when increasingly home and work became physically separated, and home became idealized as a place of refuge from the world of work. "Domesticity supposedly allowed workhorses and calculating machines to become men again, by exposing them to human rhythms and human affections."[61] But Tosh shows that there were inherent contradictions that beset men's lives as they attempted to balance time at home with their associational commitments and male friendships. Additionally domesticity and a more traditional notion of masculinity based on heroism and adventure were not entirely compatible. Domesticity, itself, was troubled by contradictions as the ideal of a companionate marriage focused on shared values and interests as well as love was at odds with the belief in absolute sexual difference. The emphasis in the period on motherhood led to tensions concerning how boys were to be raised to be men, and increasingly they were sent to boarding schools to be educated away from the feminizing atmosphere of the household. These strains mounted in the 1860s and 1870s and the appropriateness of men's domesticity became ever more subject to debate, especially as the rise of feminism threatened to usurp men's power. Toward the end of the century the lure of all-male associations grew stronger and the call of adventure became louder. "Domesticated masculinity came under mounting attack, as Englishmen were called upon to colonize the empire, and to defend it in difficult times."[62] Middle-class men began marrying later, and some men remained single. There was, Tosh argues, a "flight from domesticity."[63] Both the family histories and public discourses about marriage he examined showed that "the contradictions which had always been inherent in masculine domesticity had by the end of the century come into the open."[64]

Tosh's thesis about a "flight from domesticity" has been highly influential, but it also has been criticized. Based upon his own research and the research of other historians, Martin Francis argues that male responses to domesticity were complex throughout the nineteenth and twentieth centuries. "Men constantly travelled back and forward across the frontier of domesticity, if only in the realm of imagination, attracted by the responsibilities of marriage or fatherhood, but also enchanted by fantasies of the energetic life and homosocial camaraderie of the adventure hero."[65] A man might revel in adventure stories during one part of the day while spending another part of it playing with his children and tending the garden. Francis also criticizes the thesis that people were so appalled by the devastation and loss of life during World War I that this led to a re-domestication of masculinity. Instead, he maintains, men continued to travel backwards and forwards between imagined adventures away from home and their domestic lives. In his detailed study of RAF pilots and members of bomb crews during World War II, using first-person accounts and fiction written by men who were themselves members of the RAF, Francis reveals the significance of men's domestic worlds, especially with their families living close to the airbases where the men were stationed. He also demonstrates the significance of love and anticipated marriage for men of the RAF as they looked to a post-war future in which "the reward for sacrifice would be a material security in which romantic love and companionship would flourish."[66]

Francis' critique of the "flight from domesticity" thesis has been followed up by David B. Marshall, who examines the life of the Canadian Presbyterian minister the Reverend Charles W. Gordon, exploring how he and other men in Canada from the 1880s to the 1930s responded to the dominant cultural codes of masculinity in their daily lives. Interestingly, he found that men like Charles Gordon did seek to escape from their homes and the strains of urban living. While some men might have engaged in adventures in the Canadian wilds, Gordon went to a cottage in the wilderness with his family, spending time especially with his son. He saw this family retreat into nature as an aid fostering the son's development as an independent man. Gordon was known for promoting the idea of "imperialism, athleticism, and militarism," or what Marshall terms "imperial muscular Christianity."[67] He practiced and transmitted to his children such a "muscular Christianity" within the context of a summer family cottage. Marshall thus concludes that this escape into the wilds was not a flight from domesticity at all but rather an extension of it.

Francis' focus on how men might have lived their lives moving between supposedly contradictory masculinities raises questions about the evidence and theoretical approaches that historians have used in their analyses and the historical issues they have addressed. A great deal of the work on masculinity by gender historians has focused on codes or ideals of masculinity. Earlier in this chapter we learned both about the changing ideologies of manhood and that hegemonic forms of masculinity in a particular society at a given point in time were always contested. Histories that focus on such matters are dealing with norms, ideals, political discourses, and/or cultural prescriptions.

Recently such approaches have been challenged by historians who are concerned not with the social or cultural construction of manhood, but with mens' subjectivities. Michael Roper, for example, argues that the letters written to and from mothers and their sons on World War I battlefields provide evidence of the emotional consequences of trench warfare for participants and the significance to them of their familial relationships.[68] His analysis of letters written by regimental officers to their mothers, for example, focuses on men's psychological states as they "veered between the mother-centered existence of their early years and the precepts of manliness associated with school and the military."[69] Roper's critique has been taken up by historians like David Marshall who use a biographical method of historical analysis.

Conclusion

This chapter has sought to introduce the reader to how gender historians have approached the topic of manhood. It has presented three approaches to the subject. One focuses on the cultural codes that informed how men should be men as they lived their lives in different periods. From studies using this approach we have learned that for medieval and early modern men to be manly men or to attain the status of manhood, they had to test their manliness against other men or they had to achieve the status of manhood through marriage and becoming head of a household. We have seen that there were competing codes of manliness and different kinds of men might assert themselves as men, at times coming into open conflict, as in Bacon's Rebellion in Colonial Virginia. We have seen how violence between men and its use against children, wives, and slaves unsettled patriarchal masculinity, and conjectured that the very association of manhood (and men) with power might be at the basis of what some have referred to as a "crisis of masculinity."

Research focused on codes of masculinity and their performance by men illustrates how these codes change historically and investigates the history of men as gendered social actors. But as Mrinalini Sinha has pointed out with regard to her work on colonial masculinities discussed above, another approach to the history of masculinity or manhood understands masculinity as detached from male bodies.[70] Such an approach to codes of masculinity enables the historian to see how the meanings of masculinity are deployed to reproduce or contest particular relations of power in specific historical circumstances. Thus Sinha's analysis of colonial masculinities in British India shows how the idea of the "manly Englishman" and the "effeminate Bengali" was derived from and was used in the politics of colonial rule. Her approach is similar to that of Kristin Hoganson's research on the politics of masculinity as it played out in the debates leading to the Spanish–American and Philippine–American wars in the turn-of-the-century United States. Hoganson argued that the participants in the debate (who most likely were men) used different versions of manhood rhetorically because a convergence of factors made particular notions of masculinity especially relevant to American diplomacy.

While this chapter has focused primarily on the cultural constructions of masculinity or manliness, it has presented, however briefly, a third approach to the topic of masculinity – one that raises questions of the emotional lives of male historical actors and how cultural constructs of masculinity have been lived. This approach returns masculinity to men's bodies and concerns itself with gender subjectivity, a topic which we shall revisit in the final chapter of this book. The next chapter, meanwhile, will explore some of the research illuminating how gender has been a significant factor in processes that have been of central concern to historians, such as revolution, war, and nation formation.

5
Gender and Historical Knowledge

For the past twenty-five years or so, gender historians have demonstrated the ways in which gender has been implicated in the subjects and topics that have long been of interest to scholars. Earlier chapters covered some of this literature. We learned, for instance, about gender's centrality to the development of slavery in America and the Caribbean, and have encountered examples of how gender and sexuality have been at the heart of the relations between colonized and colonizers. This chapter will begin with an examination of the role of gender in the frequently violent struggles involving English colonists, Indians, and the French in the sixteenth- and early seventeenth-century North American borderlands. It will then explore what feminist historians have learned about the role of gender in the eighteenth-century "Age of Revolutions" and will examine issues related to those political transformations – the idea of "the nation," the gender of warfare, and the question of political citizenship.

Ann Little's research focuses on the common assumptions about gender difference shared by the English, the French, and the Indians that informed their often belligerent encounters with one another in North America from 1636 to 1763. Rather than focusing on the differences amongst these different peoples, she argues that some assumptions about gender, in particular men's roles in their respective societies, were very similar. Her research shows that it "was a universally understood insult throughout the early modern Atlantic world to call a man a woman. Nowhere in colonial America would being called a woman be understood as a compliment or a neutral comment on a man's competence or worthiness."[1] As a consequence, Indians, English, and French used gendered rhetoric in contesting each other's power and authority. In these contests, the rewards for which were agricultural lands and hunting grounds, gender and family differences were central to the language and ideology of conquest. While there were cultural differences among Indian, French, and English people, and each group insisted that such differences were crucial to their conflicts, the fact that they were fighting for political and military control heightened the import of the similar value they placed on manhood, especially men's performance in war and politics. From the beginning of the encounters between English settlers and the Indians of southern New England in the early seventeenth century, the Indians and the English both saw politics and war as men's pursuits. Indeed, all three sides, Indian, French, and English, spoke "the same gendered language of power" and knew that "it was not only their sovereignty or their livelihoods that were at stake in seventeenth- and eighteenth-century warfare; what was at stake was their very manhood."[2] Little shows, for example, that Englishmen captured by the Indians and forced to wear Indian clothes were stripped not only of their clothing but of their manhood itself. Captivity narratives written by captured Englishwomen, meanwhile, criticized Indian families in gendered terms as containing "weak men, arrogant women, and unruly children."[3] The English, moreover, used gendered language to discredit their French competitors, associating the French and their Catholicism with femininity and corruption. In sum, from the beginning of her story in 1636 to its conclusion after the English defeated the French in 1763, Little argues that gendered language and rituals were used to justify war, imperial rivalry, and subjugation in the North American borderlands.

The late eighteenth century witnessed revolutionary movements that moved back and forth across the Atlantic Ocean, involving colonists in North America, the Dutch, the Belgians, and the French in Europe, as well as slaves in the

French Caribbean, with different consequences for men and women. Born of complex economic and political determinants and influenced by the philosophical debates of the Enlightenment both on the Continent and in Britain, the events of these momentous years gave both women and men a language of liberty and equality that promised a brighter future. The immediate political consequences for them at the time, however, were substantially different.

American and French women's historians have illuminated the roles played by women in the political upheavals in their countries. In the American Revolution many women as family members followed the troops and provided them with domestic services, but their military contributions were unrecognized. Women signed petitions, joined protests, and were central to a boycott of British goods as consumers and spinners of yarn. Notable women such as Abigail Adams and especially Mercy Otis Warren, who wrote anti-British and anti-Loyalist plays, outspokenly supported the movement for independence. But such activities, while important to the conduct of the Revolution, were not of the sort that would qualify them for political citizenship in the new nation that resulted from it.

As we learned from our discussion in Chapter 4 of Anne Lombard's research on growing up male in Colonial New England, manhood was understood in relation to boyhood or dependence. Thus, in his tract *Common Sense*, Thomas Paine depicted the new America as having come of age exhibiting "the natural independence of the grown son."[4] The "sons of liberty" overthrew the patriarchal King, George III, and founded a new nation whose defense and governance would be in the hands of these newly independent men and their brothers. Women continued to be seen as dependent. But they did have a special place in the new nation. As "liberty's daughters" they were to contribute to family harmony and thus to the nation as virtuous republican mothers, especially by fulfilling their duty to raise republican sons. In Mary Beth Norton's assessment, while the new society recognized women's activities as wives and mothers to be valuable, the legacy of the American Revolution for women was ambiguous.[5] Women could only be citizens in a very restricted sense – one that was excluded from the domain of politics.

Ideas about gender difference and the characteristics of masculinity and femininity shaped the images that political actors deployed in their rebellion against the British Crown. Ruth Bloch maintains that in the early years of the revolutionary movement, the familial metaphor of Britain as the "mother country" underwent a transformation. As the conflict between the colonists and the British deepened, the "imperial mother quickly turned from tender to cruel" and the King was portrayed as a heartless father.[6] The image of tyrannical power became hyper-masculine – brutish. It was in this context that the image of "liberty" was depicted as a fragile female. But as resistance turned into rebellion, American masculinity became associated with youthful male heroism. The "term 'manly' became itself nearly synonymous with public virtue in revolutionary discourse" and contrasted with "effeminacy," signifying laziness, luxury, and cowardliness.[7] These were understandings derived from a republican tradition that valorized military virtue and stoic self-denial. Its counterpart was a feminine conception of liberty in need of protection. The alternative philosophical thought of the time, liberalism, offering the possibility of "natural rights" for all mankind, had as its founding, but unstated, assumption the idea that the "universal" man was white and male. The language of universal, natural rights eventually would be used by those previously excluded from political citizenship to make their claims for inclusion. But at the time of the founding of the new nation, the Constitution never even bothered to state that the franchise belonged only to men. It was simply assumed that women were not eligible to participate in elections or hold office. As Mary Ryan suggests, because they were "outside the circle of political protagonists, woman could represent the purest and loftiest national virtues: she impersonated the goddess of Liberty and Columbia, the icon of national unity."[8]

The gendered politics of the American Revolution and the establishment of the newly independent republic had reverberations in the realm of religious dissent, as Susan Juster's work has shown.[9] Religion may seem far removed from the protests against the British Crown that swept the colonies in the 1860s and 1870s and led to war, but evangelicals who were struggling against the established Congregational

Church drew parallels between the two movements. Before then, in the late seventeenth and eighteenth century, pious women were active in the nascent Baptist community. As Juster explains, the invigorated evangelical revivalists of the 1740s believed that all people, both women and men, could understand "spiritual truth," and importantly included women along with men in their collective governance. Furthermore, the characteristics associated with evangelical faith – emotionalism and sensuality – were at the time thought of as feminine traits. But in the late eighteenth century, as the Baptists became increasingly recognized as a legitimate Protestant denomination rather than a sect, the community attempted to shed its feminine image and adopt a more masculine face. Church governance was delegated to standing committees composed exclusively of men. The clergy became involved in revolutionary politics, encouraging patriotism among their congregations and serving as militia chaplains in the Continental army. And like the new nation brought into being by the war of independence, the Evangelical Church took on a masculine persona, "realigning the evangelical order along a more conventional male–female axis, one in line with contemporary developments in the Anglo-American world."[10] Juster's argument and the evidence she musters to support it are more complex than can be related here. But what is important for our purposes is to see how gender shaped the rhetoric producing and the consequences of the political upheavals in late eighteenth-century North America, with effects that reached beyond the political arena and throughout the fledgling American republic.

While women played active and significant roles in the early years of the evangelical movement when it was on the margins of the religious mainstream in the New England colonies, they played important but still relatively minor roles in the struggle for independence. In France, however, as feminist historians have documented, Parisian women were major players in that country's revolutionary drama, especially between 1789 and 1793.

Political upheaval in France was precipitated by an economic crisis produced by the monarchy's indebtedness following a protracted war with England and French involvement in the American Revolution. The financial crisis deepened and protests mounted in 1789. The women of Paris participated in the storming of the Bastille to seize ammunition, and took it upon themselves, as bread prices rose, to march to the royal palace at Versailles to insist that the King and Queen return to Paris to attend to the worsening economic situation. Through the years of the constitutional monarchy they participated in parades and protests and wrote petitions, one of which demanded the right of the suffrage for women, and their eligibility for public office. The National Assembly's 1791 Constitution extended the franchise to all men over 25 who met certain property qualifications, deeming them "active citizens." By contrast, all women were constructed as "passive citizens" and were prohibited from participating in politics. In 1791 as a response to the new constitution and to LaFayette's "Declaration of the Rights of Man and Citizen," Olympe de Gouges wrote the "Declaration of the Rights of Women and the Female Citizen," with a set of demands including legal protection for illegitimate children and their mothers, a role in government, female suffrage, and a separate National Assembly for women.

The monarchy was overthrown and the French Republic was established in 1792. The King, Louis XVI, was tried, convicted, and executed for treason in January 1793. Nine months later the Queen, Marie Antoinette, was also tried and executed. Women took part in both of these arrests and executions. In 1793 radical women revolutionaries established the Society of Revolutionary Republican Women and participated in the enforcement of the repressive laws of the Terror by denouncing those they believed to be counter-revolutionary. They proudly wore revolutionary dress as they walked through Paris, enhancing their visibility as political actors. Six months after its founding, however, the ruling Convention abolished the Society and forbade all women's clubs and associations, although some women actively participated in subsequent protests. Women's rights, moreover, were to become even more circumscribed under the Napoleonic regime that came to power with a coup in 1799.

The history of women's activism, their demands, and especially their exclusion from politics is important to understanding the French Revolution and its gendered consequences. But it is not the whole story of the significance of gender to the Revolution. For that it is necessary to examine the gender imagery deployed during it – imagery present in both rhetoric and visual representation.

The language and visual images circulating in France in pamphlets and cartoons and deployed by the Revolutionaries to condemn the Queen, Marie Antoinette, and justify her execution were rife with images of her sexual excess and perversity. Even before the Revolution, she was accused of using money to satisfy her sexual lust and of engaging in adultery and immoral sexual conduct. At the trial she was charged with counter-revolutionary activity and conspiring with her brother, the Austrian emperor, but most damningly, she was accused of having incest with her son. Lynn Hunt's analysis of the hostile rhetoric and imagery swirling about Marie Antoinette suggests that to the Revolutionaries, she represented "the menace of the feminine and the effeminizing to republican notions of manhood and virility."[11] She was depicted as the opposite to the virtuous nation. To the Revolutionaries, she exemplified a characteristic of the feminine more generally: she dissimulated – she was deceitful and cunning while the Revolutionaries valued transparency above all. She was a bad mother in contrast to "*La Nation*," which was depicted as a "masculine mother or father capable of giving birth."[12] The accusations against her, Hunt argues, which included promiscuity, incest, poisoning the heir to the throne, plots to replace the heir with someone who would bow to her wishes, reflect the anxiety of the time about women invading the public sphere. This anxiety became especially pronounced in the immediate aftermath of the establishment of the Republic, when women's activism was feared to be unsettling the gender order. This fear of women's participation in politics led the Convention to outlaw women's clubs and to make clear that the political sphere was to be occupied by a fraternity of men. Thus the Revolutionary slogan with the words "liberty" and "equality" depended upon a literal meaning of the third word in the motto, "fraternity."

Sexual innuendo also was used by the radical Jacobin revolutionaries against women who joined and supported the more moderate revolutionary group, the Girondins. The Jacobins taunted the Girondins with the charge that Girondin ministers were controlled by their wives. They accused politically active women of being sexually licentious, behaving like sluts, and no better than aristocratic women of the *ancien régime*. Revolutionaries often singled out women as a corrupting influence on the nation, claiming them to be frivolous and that they tended to dissimulate. Even Olympe de Gouges, who was outspoken on behalf of women's rights, said about women in the Old Regime that they

> have done more harm than good. Constraint and dissimulation have been their lot.... The French government, especially, depended throughout the centuries on the nocturnal administrations of women...ambassadorial post, command, ministry, presidency, pontificate, college of cardinals; finally, anything which characterizes the folly of men, profane and sacred, all have been subject to the cupidity and ambition of this sex, formerly contemptible and respected, and since the revolution, respectable and scorned.[13]

In essence, de Gouges was arguing that before the Revolution, women may have been respected, but they engaged in dissolute behavior and dissimulation because of their exclusion from politics and their powerlessness relative to men. But since the Revolution they had become respectable but scorned nonetheless. Ironically, however, while arguing for women's inclusion as equals in political affairs, she used some of the same negative images that the Revolutionaries had deployed against women who were politically active.

Mary Wollstonecraft in England reflected on the events occurring in France and in 1792 published an extensive analysis of their implications for women, *A Vindication of the Rights of Woman*. As its title suggests, she argued that women were capable of contributing to the public good, but that the restrictions on their education and political activities had prevented them from demonstrating their potential. She argued that women should be granted political rights and the conditions that would make them virtuous mothers. But like de Gouges, she blamed aristocratic women and their excesses for giving women a bad name.

If negative female stereotypes were so prevalent in Revolutionary France, why, then, were there so many female visual representations of the new French republic? Stylized female figures represented Liberty, Reason, Wisdom, Victory, and even Force.[14] Like Columbia in the United States, Liberty and the others were represented as female because women were *not* imagined as political actors. In other words, they were chosen to represent the virtues of the new republic because of their distance from reality. Women had never been allowed to rule in France, and so female images would not be mistaken for the patriarchal monarchy and therefore there would be no confusion as to what form of governance the allegorical female figures were representing.

Increasingly, when women were publicly represented, they were shown in motherly roles. Hunt describes parades of pregnant women and the growing emphasis by the Jacobins on "family values."[15] But there was continual criticism when live women represented the virtues in republican festivals, and using actresses, especially young women, to play the role of Liberty or Reason in a festival was condemned as inappropriate.

Were women completely disadvantaged by the Revolution? Historians continue to debate this question. Clearly, the Revolution rejected the idea that women could be actors on the stage of national politics. But as the work of Suzanne Desan argues, the Revolution challenged the patriarchy of the *ancien régime* by instituting reforms to family law benefiting women and children. Most important reforms were those that enabled divorce and mandated equal inheritance between children. The incidence of divorce after the law was passed in 1792 varied, being highest in cities and towns and lower in smaller communities. Generally it was women who initiated the divorce, primarily to end marriages that had already been fractured by desertion or violence. In the rhetoric of the Revolution, Desan maintains that "the natural bonds of conjugal love and family unity assumed ever greater importance as an imagined source of political transformation as well as social cohesion."[16] Focusing on the province of Normandy as a case study, she shows that deploying Revolutionary rhetoric about the family and using the new laws, women and illegitimate children made claims for greater independence and control over property. But these reforms were to be short-lived. In reaction to the liberalization of domestic life, the reactionary Convention of 1795 abolished the laws on egalitarian inheritance and divorce, paving the way for the more gender-restrictive measures brought into law with the Napoleonic Code of 1804. Thus although women did not gain equality with men when it came to political participation during the Revolutionary period in France, debates over rights gave women, however temporarily, one arena in which to challenge their position in society. Moreover, across Europe in the Dutch Republic, Belgium, and areas of Italy and Germany, the issue of women's political rights was debated. In the much longer run the universal language of political rights made possible arguments for women's rights.

At the time, however, the outcome of both the American and French Revolutions as well as the political upheavals that spread out from them across Europe as in the Dutch Republic resulted in the masculinizing of the political sphere. While women were either denigrated as symbolizing the ills of the monarchy and/or envisioned as potential republican mothers, conceptions of manhood were critical to the reshaping of political citizenship.

As we have seen in the foregoing discussion, the meanings of femininity and masculinity and their connection to politics both shaped and were reshaped during the Age of Revolutions. Sharply drawn social divisions of gender and race supported by a growing orthodoxy of "natural" or biological differences were fundamental to the creation of modern Western society in the late eighteenth and early nineteenth centuries, although those same revolutions stimulated debates about gender, race, and political rights that would continue through much of the twentieth.

There were other long-lasting outcomes of the Age of Revolutions. Importantly, the political upheavals of the late eighteenth century gave birth to the modern idea of "nation" and its close associate, nationalism. Most scholars agree that the "nation" is an invented category which, from the Age of Revolutions, came to mean a unified and sovereign "people." Nations are, in Benedict Anderson's terms, "imagined communities." They are imagined as unique and bounded by what the members of the community have in common, be it language, "history," or presumed ethnic roots.[17] The idea of the national "community" is imagined because its members do not know one another but yet they feel a sense of common identity with one another. Nationalism, a powerful ideology, makes claims for sovereignty – that "the political and the national unit should be congruent."[18]

The American Revolution, like the French Revolution, was waged to overthrow a monarchy and to establish a republic. But it also was a war of independence – a war that would establish the thirteen colonies of Britain as a separate and sovereign state. We have already seen that gender was central to both of these revolutionary movements, and that gender imagery was critical to the establishment of the new nations that resulted from them. Moreover, feminist scholars have shown the significance of gender to nationalist movements as nationalism spread across Europe and through imperialism to the rest of the world.

We have also seen with the example of the French Revolution that the nation created by it was forged through the "sanctioned institutionalization of gender difference."[19] Women and men were imagined as "naturally" different kinds of citizens with different and unequal rights. Both the American and the French Revolutions purposefully disrupted the previous patriarchal political order by overthrowing the King and replacing him with a fraternity – the sons of liberty. These revolutions upset the social order and it was then the responsibility of the new governments to reestablish orderly societies. One means by which this happened was again through reasserting gender difference and idealizing a particular form of family life – one in which the republican mother was given a central role.

Gendered familial imagery has been shown to play a central role in the construction of the imagined community of the nation. The terms referring to the territory that the nation-state inhabits suggest this. Countries are known as the "motherland," "mother country," "fatherland," and, in Germany, as *heimat*, meaning home or homeland. The language of kinship depicts citizens of the nation as daughters or sons. Fathers, mothers, and uncles all make their appearance in national stories and images. Familial language lends to the nation the belief that it is a "natural" organic community. Like a family, the ties between its members are thought to be instinctive – based on blood and/or a deep ancestral history. Familial images provide the nation with a sense of unity, but it is a unity based upon hierarchies of gender, race, and class. They legitimate the nation and its hierarchical divisions as "natural" just as the family with its gender and age hierarchy is a supposedly "natural form." In Venezuela, for example, the patriarchal family was a metaphor for national unification, with women, whose role was to be reproducers in the family and the "mother of the nation," seen as dependants in both realms.[20] But as Mrinalini Sinha has emphasized, the family form that accompanied the history of the nation is a specific one – the heterosexual, bourgeois nuclear family – privileging marriage between one woman and one man and particular norms of sexual respectability.[21]

A number of scholars have suggested that familial metaphors and female images in nationalist discourse arouse emotional attachment to the nation. In Revolutionary France, as Joan Landes has argued, the "family came to be associated with the values of intimacy and sentimentality, and private morality was seen as a necessary condition for a healthy state and society."[22] Furthermore, representing the nation as a female, she suggests, worked to stimulate passions of love and possession on the part of the male citizen who was duty-bound to protect it. The preamble of the Constitution passed in 1795 tied good citizenship for men to family life and honorable behavior: "No one is a good citizen if he isn't a good son, good father, good brother, good friend, good spouse."[23] In Iran at the end of the nineteenth century, nationalist writers using imagery of love transformed what had been sentiments connected to Islamic faith and the divine into devotion to the national homeland, the *vatan*. They used language that had once been associated with classical male homoerotic poetry to transform the *vatan* into a female object of love, the "beloved." The *vatan* also was figured as mother, especially in literature that spoke of defending the honor and integrity of Iran. As Asfenah Najmabadi argues, "The trope of *vatan* as mother thus rearticulated the duties of children toward their parents into duties of (male) citizens toward mother *vatan*."[24] Devotion to Iran in patriotic discourse was linked both to a female lover and to a maternal figure, and these images and the sentiments they aroused were instrumental in the creation of Iran as a modern nation.

Concerns about family life formed a "basic framework through which abstract concepts such as nation, and, along with it, loyalty and citizenship were imagined, articulated, and debated by Egyptians from the inception of the modern Egyptian nation-state in the early nineteenth century"[25] and on through to the early twentieth. In Egypt, as they did in other parts of Africa and in India, the British justified their occupation, beginning in 1882, by asserting that the nature of the people's family life proved their political backwardness. But, long before then changes in home life and marriage among the elite were taking place and served as a means by which bourgeois Egyptians could distinguish themselves from the Ottoman Turks who had dominated Egypt before it became a semi-autonomous principality of the Ottoman Empire. From the early nineteenth century as a result of educational reforms, elite children were exposed to Western institutions and ideologies, including those related to marriage and motherhood. In the two decades prior to the British occupation, there had been substantial transformation in the family lives of the bourgeoisie.[26] The familial images in British colonizing discourse thus melded with a vision of the significance of family life to the political nation that was "home-grown," albeit influenced by European ideas about modernity. By the early twentieth century, discussions about the significance of the domestic realm were reflected in a "gendered, feminine 'Mother Egypt.'" This new way of depicting Egypt provided an image of a motherland that was home to Egyptians from different classes and language groups, providing them with "a common heritage, a common lineage, and a common connection to the struggle of ousting the British."[27] Nationalists then used the Egyptian bourgeois family ideal to signify their readiness for independence from the British and domestic imagery proliferated as demonstrations in 1919 led to revolution. They also used the concept of family honor as a way to strengthen national pride and its violation by the nation's occupiers. For example, after British soldiers raped village women in 1919, the incident became known first as the "rape of 'our women'" and then the "rape of the nation, a dishonor shared by the collective."[28] But the family politics of the revolution had different consequences for men and women. Although women were active in the movement for independence, they were excluded from decision-making in public affairs and were relegated to their symbolic role as "mothers of Egypt."

Family reform and the status of women were touchstones of modernity and nation building in twentieth-century Turkey and were integral to revolution and nation formation in China. In the case of Turkey, Europeanization was critical to the modernizing policies of Mustafa Kemal, who ousted the European forces occupying Turkey after they had defeated the Ottomans in World War I, abolished the Sultanate, and then established the Turkish Republic in 1923. Kemal, or Atatürk as he was named, meaning "father of the people," became its president. Both family reform and the emancipation of women from orthodoxy were central to his vision of the new Turkish nation. He supported secular education for women, believing their education would be in the best interests of the nation's children. While stressing the importance of motherhood for women, he condemned men's dominance of family life. The new government abolished divorce by renunciation and polygamy, and gave women equal rights pertaining to divorce and inheritance. In a sense, then, a reformed domestic sphere and the advancement of women's status came to symbolize the modern nation brought into being by Atatürk, the nation's father.[29]

The family, "women's emancipation," and nationalism were dramatically linked in twentieth-century China's revolutionary politics. In the late nineteenth and early twentieth century, reformers who were reacting to threats from Western and Japanese imperialists called for reform of traditional Chinese institutions to bring the country into the modern world. They were influenced by various intellectual trends in the West in their analysis of the ills afflicting China. It was especially during what was known as the New Culture Movement, beginning in 1915 and lasting for eight years (also known as the May Fourth Movement), that educated urban youth began a vociferous attack on China's traditional culture. The young radicals were spurred by the Chinese government's relinquishing of economic power to Japan in 1915 and in 1919 to the Versailles Treaty, which had ceded to the Japanese an area of China formerly under the control of Germany. Like their predecessors, they looked to the West for models of social and political organization. The traditional, joint, patriarchal family (formed by arranged marriages, with the son's wife and their children living in the household of the son's parents) and the status of women were particularly thought to be detrimental to China's national interests. The radicals wished to replace the traditional family with a Western-style family model involving free choice of marriage partners, companionate marriage, and independence from their kin. They believed that a new kind of family would help to build a revitalized nation. According to historian Susan Glosser, the purpose of the small or conjugal family was to "instill the independence, productivity, and civic concern that the beleaguered state needed."[30] She suggests that the radicals of the New Culture Movement prescribed these revisions in family life basing them on and articulating them within time-honored Chinese beliefs that the strength of the state depended upon the family. The family and women's roles within it were to be recast in order to rebuild the nation. In other words, New Culture radicals envisioned a new form of family that would enhance the quality of individuals' private lives *in the interest of the nation* not as an end in itself. This formulation, Glosser shows, influenced the family policies of the Nationalist government in the 1930s and then the policies of the People's Republic in the 1950s as the state increased its control over the conjugal family in the interest of the nation.

In China, as in Atatürk's Turkey, women's traditional roles were believed to be ill suited to a modern nation. From the late nineteenth century, reformers maintained that China's traditional culture not only crippled women's bodies by the practice of footbinding, but also their minds by depriving them of education and contact with the world outside of their households. In the aftermath of the Revolution of 1911 that overthrew the Qing dynasty (1644–1912) and established a republican government, a small but vociferous women's suffrage movement came into being, although it was short-lived. However, with the New Culture Movement, "women's emancipation came to symbolize a critical distinction between 'feudal' China and China as a 'modern' nation-state."[31] These ideas influenced the intellectuals who joined the Nationalist Party founded by Sun Yatsen in 1920 and the

Communist Party founded in 1921 on the heels of the May Fourth protests of 1919. Men in the Communist Party dominated the feminist discourse that flourished in these years, joining feminism to Marxism and both to the transformation of the nation. These ideals undoubtedly encouraged women to join the party and to actively espouse the idea of women's emancipation and family reform, although the gender hierarchy within the party remained male-dominated. Communist women as well as men accepted that women's primary responsibilities to the nation were to act as mothers and wives.

So far in this chapter we have seen the relationship between gender, revolution, and the idea of the nation. It is important to keep in mind that one reason that gender was so important to eighteenth-century revolutionary processes is that "[t]he 'age of democratic revolutions' ushered in an era in which major political transformations were preceded by, resulted from, or ended in war."[32] And it is only in the very recent past in Europe and North America that combatants were not supposed to be exclusively male. It is no wonder then that warfare has been highly gendered.

Classical republicanism was central to the American Revolutionaries as they arose to establish an independent republic. The conception of citizenship fundamental to classical republicanism revolved around the idea of the citizen-soldier whose manly independence guaranteed his virtue. While the nature of the military organization, whether it was to be made up of volunteer militias or a conscripted force, was a critical debate during the period, the manly political ideal of the virtuous citizen-soldier was crucial to the American Revolution and to the republic that was built in its aftermath.

Similarly in France male civic virtue was linked to the idea of the citizen-soldier. There too a debate about the nature of military organization took place. Yet the "conflation of male citizenship and military service increasingly virilised masculinity, differentiating it ever more emphatically from femininity."[33] The decreeing of the *levée en masse* in August 1793 by the Revolutionary government that envisioned all male persons serving the military in some capacity furthered the figure of the citizen-soldier as central to the new fraternal political and social order.

But it was the Napoleonic Era in France that witnessed the cultivation of a martial masculinity for Frenchmen in line with the regime's belligerent world-wide imperial ambitions. Whereas the Revolutionaries had attempted to downplay the heroic notions of manhood associated with the French aristocracy, after Napoleon secured control of the government of France in 1799, the regime promulgated the ideal of virile, aggressive, and consummately heterosexual masculinity for all men. According to historian Michael J. Hughes, Napoleon understood French men to be naturally warlike.[34] Especially nobles were claimed to be natural warriors, and he reestablished aristocratic values in the army. The regime recruited tens of thousands of men into the army who were expected to return after their military service to their families to raise sons to be virile soldiers. As Napoleon's armies swept across the Western world, femininity was thought to be characterized by "faint-heartedness," women were portrayed as downcast as their loved ones marched off to war, and images of French soldiers' sexual conquests proliferated. The self-image of France as a "hyper-masculine warrior nation" persisted through much of the nineteenth century.

While engaging in battle was a masculine privilege throughout much of Western history, there are historical examples throughout of women engaging in battle in male garb. In the fight of (Germanic) Prussia against Napoleon between 1806 and 1815, for example, at least twenty-two women joined the army dressed as men. According to Karen Hagemann's analysis, they were met with suspicion and aroused profound public ambivalence in spite of their feats in battle.[35] Both in France and in Prussia some women, aroused by patriotic sympathies, demanded the right to defend themselves and their countries (as women), but they were totally rejected. Femaleness and combat apparently were so irreconcilable that the display of unambiguous female strength was more threatening to the sense of the nation at war than were crossdressed women.

But war has not just been fought on the battlefields, especially the two world wars of the twentieth century, known as "total wars." The term "total war" suggests wars that are both extensive and devastatingly destructive, and importantly that they dissolve the boundaries between the battlefront and the home front.[36] Although women have been denied a role in combat, the world wars of the twentieth century opened spaces for women to contribute to their nation's efforts. Nicoletta Gullace has shown how women's activities in World War I Britain enabled them to claim and for some of them to win the right to political citizenship, given the close association in political thought between the ability to wage war and the qualifications for citizenship. There is a voluminous historical literature documenting and analyzing the campaign for women's suffrage in Britain as well as across the world which it would be impossible to cover here because of limitations of space. The struggle for women to obtain the vote in Britain was long and hard-fought and, as Gullace shows, the sacrifices of mothers and wives, their wartime work, and the patriotism publicly demonstrated by suffragists changed public attitudes in favor of their winning the vote. This was especially the case because while women were fully engaged in the war at home, male pacifists chose not to serve. Furthermore, as Gullace points out, previously (for reasons too complex to discuss here), the common professional soldier had been denied the vote. Given the elevation of the common soldier to the status of hero, and the castigation of both those men who refused to volunteer and those who, when conscripted, refused to serve, public support for broadening the suffrage became evident by 1918, when the Representation of the People bill was passed. Because there were men who refused either to volunteer or to serve, Gullace argues gender could no longer differentiate qualifications for the vote. The rhetoric of sacrifice for the nation was gender-neutral. Conscientious objectors, in this environment became the "symbolic and literal embodiment of the non-citizen."[37]

While in Britain, World War I made service rather than gender *per se* the mark of the citizen who could vote, prior to 1918, not all men were qualified to belong to the political nation. The struggle for universal male suffrage was both long and hard-fought. From the mid-seventeenth century through to the late nineteenth century, according to Matthew McCormack, it centered on the question of what qualified a person to count as an "independent man."

His research shows that while notions of the significance of independence to political thought and electoral reform persisted, the meanings of independence changed over the course of the late eighteenth and early nineteenth centuries and were drawn upon in the debates leading to the Great Reform Act of 1832.

The "independent man" was defined in opposition both to women and to "dependent men." Prior to the last decades of the eighteenth century, independence generally was associated with men of high societal rank and landed property. The opposite of independence was dependency, believed to make people corruptible and untrustworthy. Those who were dependent on patrons, employers, landlords, or charity lacked manliness, virtue, and free will. Over the course of the eighteenth and nineteenth centuries, McCormack argues, while citizenship continued to be judged through the lens of independence, independence increasingly became associated with gender rather than rank and the possession of landed property. Although independence remained important as a qualification for citizenship, it was "subject to redefinition and debate."[38]

In the aftermath of the Age of Revolutions, especially as radical thinkers in Britain encountered the political culture of 1770s America, a growing number of political radicals and reformers began to view political entitlement more broadly, and independence, while critical, increasingly was conceived in terms of what they considered male character traits – "sincere sensibility, rationality, humble virtues, and inherent rights."[39] At the same time, these political radicals were profoundly misogynistic. They made it clear that in no way could a woman be thought to possess such qualities. McCormack shows that the qualifications for manly independence continued to be debated through the first decades of the nineteenth century. With the extensive participation of working men, radicals made the claim that manhood itself should be the only qualification for the vote. The reformers of 1830–2 "valorised the male stations of father, husband and householder [as] the public role of independent men was predicated upon having people dependent upon them."[40]

Anna Clark's important work *The Struggle for the Breeches* also traces the changes in ideas by political radicals about citizenship for working men from the late eighteenth century, when radical artisans promulgated notions of fraternity as they dealt with the contradiction between their demands for citizenship and their lack of property. Like McCormack, Clark sees this as a masculinist radicalism which reformers by the early 1820s judged to be ineffective. She suggests that working-class or plebian radicals then transformed their notions of manhood from misogynistic to protective of and responsible for their wives and children.[41]

The agitation for electoral reform in the period leading to the 1832 Reform Act was waged by working- and middle-class men with the support of some aristocratic women. Working-class women also were present in substantial numbers in demonstrations, but women and men were represented differently in the campaigns. Men demanded their right to vote as independent men. Women were positioned in their roles as wives and mothers. Before 1832 there was no mention of women at all when it came to political rights. But in the context of the political aspirations raised by feminists such as Mary Wollstonecraft in the revolutionary climate of the 1790s, the act that was passed in 1832 formally denied women the franchise. Furthermore, not all men were eligible to vote. Newly enfranchised voters were middle-class men whose independence was demonstrated by their ownership of taxable property. Property stood in for, and was the measure of, independence or trustworthiness – in other words, it was the measure of manhood for inclusion in the political nation.[42]

But the fight for universal manhood suffrage in Britain was only just beginning. Chartism, the massive working-class movement for the vote and against economic exploitation, flourished between 1838 and the mid-1840s. Chartists argued for universal manhood suffrage, basing their claims upon the assertion that had long been made by artisans that as skilled workers, they possessed property. They had property in their labor. Thus they used a language that emphasized independence as the basis for political inclusion but broadened the meaning of property. During this period those who opposed giving the franchise to working-class men claimed that they were unruly workers and bad husbands, making it irrelevant that they had property in their labor. In other words, they began to redefine the kind of manliness that would qualify working-class men for the suffrage. They needed to be respectable men. In response, as Anna Clark has emphasized, working-class men used the ideology of domesticity, which had become so central to the middle classes, to assert their need for a breadwinner's wage so that they could support their families. And they emphasized the virtues of labor and self-improvement to claim respectability. Increasingly, Clark shows, Chartists used the economic demand for a bread-winner's wage to argue for the inclusion of working men in the political nation. Their campaign for manhood suffrage, therefore, was predicated on domesticity for women.

As the debate about the suffrage resumed in the 1860s, reformers "overlaid the idea of property in labour with cultural distinctions which differentiated between forms of working-class masculinity – between a sober, respectable and independent manhood and those 'rough' men."[43] Such debates led to the passage of the 1867 Reform Act, which extended the franchise to male householders and lodgers paying more than ten pounds rent annually. As Keith McClelland has written, the working-class man included in the franchise in 1867 "was a particular kind of man whose definition – the social, political and moral qualities he was thought to carry, his perceived relationship to the processes of government and politics – was crucial to the redefinition of what the political nation was and might become."[44] Respectable men, tax-paying, regularly employed working men who supported their households, possessed the kind of independent manhood that qualified them for political citizenship in the nation. In Britain it was not until 1918 that all men over the age of 21 could vote. The Representation of the People Act of 1918 granted the vote only to women over the age of 30. Equal suffrage for women and men was still a decade away.

Conclusion

This chapter has introduced the reader to how analyzing gender has helped to illuminate major political transformations. Our discussion of gender and revolution have traversed a period of history beginning with the eighteenth-century Age of Revolutions, and the gendering of citizenship that resulted. We have examined how gendered imagery was used to represent the nation formed by those revolutions, and the ways that family life and gender were of significance to twentieth-century political transformations across the world. We have learned that gendered imagery and familial sentiment were crucial in different kinds of nation-building efforts in the United States, France, Egypt, Turkey, Iran, China, and Venezuela. The chapter has examined how the study of gender contributed to historical discussion about war and has explored the connection between war and political citizenship. Our discussion has ended with a focus on changing understandings of what kind of manhood was thought necessary for the acquisition of political rights in nineteenth-century Britain and the continued exclusion of all women until 1928.

Significant historical work also has been done on gender, labor, and industrial transformation in both capitalist and socialist economies. This book will include some examples of this literature in the suggested readings. The final chapter, meanwhile, examines debates over approaches to gender history and introduces the reader to some new directions in the field.

6

Assessing "Turns" and New Directions

The rise and growth of gender history from about the mid-1980s through the 1990s accompanied and contributed to what has variously been called the "linguistic turn," post-structuralism, and post-modernism. Each of these designations has its own philosophical and/or theoretical roots and analytical specificities, although they have frequently been seen as part of the same general movement in history. Separately and together they led historians to question the nature of their discipline. At the very beginning of this book the reader encountered a definition of history that is at the center of what I will tentatively refer to as a "post-modernist" understanding of the nature of the discipline. We only know the past through the historian's construction of it. Historians gather evidence – various traces of the lives lived before the present, referred to as "documents" – and then interpret that evidence. They then shape their interpretations into depictions of the past. Thus our access to the past, to what "really happened," is mediated by layers of interpretation, all involving the use of language and the attribution of meaning. We might know that a certain event took place, but establishing how it happened, who participated, and evaluating its consequences involve reading its traces.

While to some extent earlier historians had assumed that they were active producers of the past, the post-modern "turn" among historians in the closing decades of the twentieth century increased sensitivity to and appreciation of the importance of questioning the grounds of historical knowledge. And, as Geoff Eley and Keith Nield have written, "it opens the way for multiple standpoints. Because the past cannot be definitively reclaimed or reconstructed, and the past's totality is irrecoverable, our access to understanding will necessarily remain...provisional."[1] History is always subject to revision and contestation. And as we shall see, there are new strands of historical analysis both within gender history and outside of it that are opening new pathways of inquiry. But before discussing these newer trends, it is important to see how gender history has been engaged with the post-modern, post-structuralist linguistic turn.

Kathleen Canning has argued that feminist history generally was central to its development.[2] As she suggests, feminist scholars in the 1970s and 1980s rejected the idea that biology explained sexual inequalities, and argued that sexual difference was socially constructed. The whole thrust of gender history was to undermine the idea that the subjects of history were disembodied white men, so that from its beginnings it was involved in destabilizing history as it had traditionally been practiced. The feminist historians who took the "linguistic turn" went further by placing language and discourse at the center of their examination of how gender was constituted and how it influenced historical processes. They understood language and discourse as constituting historical "reality" – constructing it rather than simply reflecting it. This unsettled and disturbed other feminist historians, who objected to the idea that everything was constructed through language, giving the impression that there was no reality apart from "the text" or what was written about it. Some were concerned that this new history would lead into an abyss of relativism that negated progressive feminist politics. Others claimed that discourse or language became a new master category that supposedly explained everything rather than being one component "in the making of social relations and their histories."[3]

Debate among feminist historians as well as among historians more generally raged in the 1990s and became referred to as the "theory wars," which took place not only in scholarly journals but also in more "mainstream" media.[4] It was particularly the influence of the ideas of Michel Foucault and Jacques Derrida that stimulated debate. To Foucault and those who followed him, power in modern societies is dispersed rather than centrally located. It is intrinsically bound up with knowledge. Thus in the history of sexuality, sex became an object of scientific disciplines, and those disciplines and the knowledge that they produced served as instruments of control. Moreover, knowledge controls by being internalized by individuals who use it as a basis of self-knowledge and, thus, self-control. Critics worried that such a discursive understanding of power denied or ignored domination as well as the material economic or social constraints that influenced people's lives.

Jacques Derrida is associated with deconstructionism, a way of understanding and reading texts. Fundamentally, his work suggested that texts can never definitively establish meaning because they are constructed by an endless play of signifiers. Western tradition attempted to claim certainty and truth by repressing that instability. But the binaries (light/dark, nature/culture, man/woman) that make up texts in this tradition are actually composed as hierarchies, such that the central term assumes the marginal one and is therefore contaminated by it. Thus texts contain internal contradictions that undermine their claims to truth or to unique meanings. Derrida's work suggested a way of reading the texts constituting historical evidence to uncover their internal contradictions and to reveal what they have suppressed – that is, to read for what has been left out or silenced. While welcomed by some historians as a way of approaching texts, others vilified Derridean post-structuralism for its singular focus on language, its own use of dense prose, and for ignoring or considering irrelevant the historical and social contexts in which particular discourses emerged.

Joan Scott was a central figure in the development of gender history, especially through her promotion of a theoretical approach to the topic of gender in history. But because of her debt to theorists such as Foucault and Derrida, and her insistence upon an exclusively post-structuralist approach to history, her ideas fueled heated debate among gender and women's historians.[5] Although a number of feminist historians lined up on one side or the other in such scholarly battles over theory, there were also gender historians who attempted to forge a "middle way" that adopted some aspects of post-structuralism while attempting to bring into their analysis questions of social context as well as the agency or the role of historical actors in contesting, resisting, or transforming the discourses that defined them and grappling with the social constraints in which they found themselves.

For example, Judith Walkowitz's *City of Dreadful Delight: Narratives of Sexual Danger in Late-Victorian London* combined Foucault's insights into discursive practices with questions from social history and feminist politics.[6] The author analyzed the changing social landscape of London in the 1880s, which encouraged a variety of different kinds of investigations into the city, including social reformers, middle-class and elite male spectators, and journalists like W. T. Stead with his sensational reports of girls sold into prostitution. These intertwined and often conflicting discourses led to political demonstrations, a bill in parliament, and increased police surveillance. Walkowitz details the social consequences of the proliferation of sexual narratives and investigates the role and impact of the media in shaping the construction of heterosexuality. And she argues that one of the results of the media frenzy over the Jack the Ripper murders was to refashion gender meanings focused on a vision of male violence and female passivity as well as to reframe images of the social landscape of the city itself. Walkowitz's work thus places discourses within a social context and assesses their social, cultural, and political effects.

In essays published in the 1990s Kathleen Canning developed an approach to gender history that emphasizes the interaction or interdependence of discourse and social context that allows for the reintroduction into gender history of notions of "experience" and agency. Central to her approach is an understanding of "the body" as being located at a "crossroads between material culture and subjectivity," such that "bodily experiences of desire and deprivation shape subjectivity in important ways."[7] So, for example, in her case study of women's labor politics in Germany after World War I she unravels the social conditions that women workers faced during wartime, their newly acquired position in a labor union, changing discourses about female bodies and women's work, and women's agency in using these discourses in political protest. Canning argues that the war years and the political and social upheavals in their immediate aftermath constituted a period in which women's embodied experiences of "hunger, stealing, striking, demonstrating, birthing or aborting opened the way for the transformations of consciousness and experience."[8] Furthermore, during the war, government policing of women's activities intensified, leading women to be more acutely aware of their special needs. In its aftermath, women's maternal bodies were the objects of widespread anxieties about population loss and quality. And it was in that complex discursive and social context that women inserted into their political demands their everyday experiences, which included intensive household labor as well as factory work, both necessary for family survival. They also spoke of their "vulnerability to illness, injury or rape...the danger and death associated with illegal abortion and the persistently high rates of infant mortality among working-class families."[9] While, before the war, arguments about women's special needs focused on the woman worker as mother, in the mid-1920s women represented themselves in their multiple roles to demand social welfare measures that addressed their specificity as women workers. This is a necessarily complex story – one that takes into account discourse, social context, agency, and experience to suggest a way of doing gender history using post-structuralism and its concern with discourse and combining it with an analysis of the material contexts about which those discourses speak. The works of Judith Walkowitz and Kathleen Canning are examples of historical scholarship that treads something of a middle path to exploit the benefits of different theoretical approaches to gender history during the time that the debate about the "linguistic turn" raged in the academy.

There is no question that interdisciplinary approaches have been indispensable in doing gender history. At this point in our discussion it might be useful to consider them as making up what Peter Burke has termed "the new cultural history," which encompasses an eclectic variety of approaches that include and may have been influenced by post-structuralism but are not reducible to it.[10] Indeed most of the studies discussed in this book make use of or are engaged with some aspect of "the new cultural history." Arguably this would include the studies of the significance of the gendered imagery influencing the course of the French Revolution discussed in Chapter 5 as well as studies such as Kathleen Brown's analysis of gender and slavery in colonial Virginia, discussed in Chapter 3. While the so-called "theory wars" may have been waged by historians who adopted radically different points of view with regard to what history should be and how it should be written, most gender historians drew their analytical tools from a plurality of traditions. Recent reflections on the state of history by historians suggest not only this pluralism but also a concerted attempt to combine cultural and social historical approaches using discourse analysis, assessing their social or historical contexts, and including a conception of the regularities through which both social opportunities and inequalities are distributed and maintained.[11]

Up to this point in our discussion, except for a brief discussion of Kathleen Canning's work, little attention has been paid to the issue of subjectivity. For Canning, the body – its physical stresses and desires – shapes subjectivity. She also sees subjectivity in terms of "subject positions" in discourse and the self-representations that these make possible.[12] For Michael Roper, whose research on the letters written by men on the battlefield to their mothers was mentioned in Chapter 4, subjectivity is concerned with psychological states. In an essay provocatively entitled "Slipping Out of View: Subjectivity and Emotion in Gender History," he is in fact, sharply critical of understandings of subjectivity that conceptualize it as subject positions in discourse. He insists instead on distinguishing between how actors use discourse and the question of psychological effects.[13] He argues against the linguistic approach to gender as theorized by Joan Scott, on several grounds. Roper maintains that excluding any notion of lived experience from a theory of gender makes an analysis of subjectivity impossible, and he objects to the idea that discourses or cultural representations constitute subjects. He argues, too, that gender history under Scott's influence has been too narrowly focused on gender as a means of constituting or signifying power, and it was "this part of the model that allowed the reach into spheres where gender did not appear to be the issue."[14] In other words, Roper sees as a problem what some gender historians would consider the strength of gender analysis for its contribution to historical understanding. Roper argues that missing from gender history is attention to "the practices of everyday life; of human experience formed through emotional relationships with others; and of that experience as involving a perpetual process of managing emotional impulses, both conscious and unconscious, within the self and in relation to others."[15] In his research on men and masculinity in World War I he attended to the everyday practices that mothers engaged in on behalf of their sons that in emotionally important ways signaled to them their love and support, such as writing, baking, sending clothing and gifts. The analysis of the letters exchanged between sons and mothers allowed him to reconstruct the emotional meaning of familial relationships. It was these relationships that were at the center of his study of masculinity, understood "as a psychic as well as a social and cultural construct."[16] Roper's is a biographical approach to history, one that draws heavily on psychoanalysis, giving the historian insight into the "psychic depth of relationships formed within the family" and their relevance in particular historical circumstances.[17]

A recent book by Timothy Ashplant uses a biographical or life history approach to explore the complex subjectivities of men during the period of the Great War. Ashplant uses three detailed case studies of men from upper-middle-class backgrounds to examine the fates of their individual and social identities as they confronted and lived with the exigencies of the brutal war on the Western Front. His purpose is not to provide a summary or portrait of how men were emotionally affected by the war, but rather to explore the formation and transformation of the social and political identities of the men as individuals. The book examines their individual personal development in their families, in the educational institutions they attended, and in the military. Ashplant's particular interest is in whether, when, and in what ways the men "negotiated, resisted or rejected their expected roles," and he focuses his attention on the impact of the war.[18] He understands the formation of personal identity as both psychic and social. He sees them as intertwined, "so that the acquisition of an adult identity is simultaneously gender-, class- and nation-specific"[19] and formed over the course of a person's life into adulthood. He also importantly examines what he refers to as "social collectivities" such as the nation and how they make demands that call upon the emotional attachments formed earlier in life as people grow into adulthood. Finally, he examines the war as a moment of disruption, or what he terms a "liminal" time and space, producing the possibility for individual transformation. The book details how World War I challenged upper-middle-class masculinity, leading some men who had previously rebelled against their upbringing to accommodate to the demands of society, while it prompted others to question and challenge what they had previously accepted.

Ashplant's work brings psychoanalytic, cultural, and social methods together to explore a history of subjectivities that takes into account the specificity of social contexts along with psychodynamics. Approaches to the history of masculinities, such as Ashplant's and Roper's, that focus on individual subjectivity are quite different to the kinds of gender history examined elsewhere in this book. Examining subjectivity from the perspective of the individual psyche (understood as being formed within specific historical contexts) offers a new direction in gender history, although psychoanalytic approaches to history, *per se*, are not new. In a way, like early women's history and the social history that influenced it, this approach is an effort at "recovery." As Ashplant remarks, like histories intended to "recover and make audible the voices of those [who, had been] excluded from the centres of power and cultural authority," work such as his is meant to recover " 'voices within'... the inner conflicts, the contradictory voices at work within individuals."[20] Ashplant's approach is an amalgam of several ways of thinking about gender history, intended, as he puts it, "to illuminate the interaction of... forces – individual and social; psychological, cultural, and material – which gives rise to these conflicts."[21]

But are such approaches that attempt to recover subjectivity using a psychoanalytic perspective limited to modern histories? Lyndal Roper has argued that while early modern people may have thought differently about mind and body, the processes of identity formation are enduring. Identity, she argues, using psychoanalytic reasoning, is formed "in part through identification with – and separation from – others, a feature which does not set the early modern period apart."[22] Her understanding of gendered subjectivity is grounded in her assessment of the significance of the sexed body to history. Sexual difference, she argues, is not merely "social. It is also physical."[23] Psychoanalysis allows for an analysis of the interdependence of the psychic and the physical and its consequences for subjectivity. Roper sees individual subjectivities exposed in witch trials, as the transcripts reveal that the accused and accusers, all of whom were women, focused especially on bodily concerns of motherhood and infancy or expressed their rage against parental authority. She understands the phenomenon of witchcraft in seventeenth-century Germany as related to "the psychic conflicts attendant on the feminine position" as they were expressed through the cultural narratives of the time. In other words, Roper sees culture as shaping how an individual's underlying subjectivities or emotional states are expressed.

A focus on subjectivity and emotion is one approach to the study of gender history that appears to be gaining momentum. There are also other trends in historical practice that lead in seemingly quite different directions. At about the time that gender history was developing along with the new cultural history, other historians became increasingly interested in what has been called world or global history. Widespread interest in and concerns about contemporary globalization and a recognition of the significance of non-Western histories to social, economic, and cultural transformations that have affected societies across the globe have spurred interest in world/global/international history. Generally, histories of women and gender have not figured in the practice of world or global history. And although histories of women and gender have been written about societies across the world, historians of women and gender have not until recently adopted a "world history" approach. World or global history and women's and gender history appear to have developed along separate and non-intersecting tracks. This, however, has begun to change as an increasing number of gender and women's historians have heeded the call to think more globally, and, in turn, a small number of world historians have attended to gender.

One possible reason for the inattention to gender by scholars of world/global history may be because of the scale of the phenomena of interest to some practitioners of the field.[24] Historians interested in explaining global economic transformations investigate societal-level social and economic forces. Using comparative analysis they examine factors that distinguish one region from another in terms of economic factors and/or they investigate flows of trade and resources across the globe and the various connections between regions. A prime example of a highly praised work in the field is Kenneth Pomeranz's *The Great Divergence: China, Europe, and the Making of the Modern World Economy*.[25] Pomeranz asks why there was a dramatic leap by Europe, especially Britain, in contrast to Asia, especially China, in the nineteenth century, in the growth of its industrial economy. He shows that Britain and China were remarkably similar in economic and social indicators that contributed to economic growth in the early modern period, but in the nineteenth century, Europe's industrial economy began to far outpace the rest of Eurasia. His explanation for the "great divergence" in the nineteenth century uses not only comparative methods – Britain's coal deposits were conveniently close to the industrial centers, making the use of steam power economically feasible, whereas China's were not. He also examines a set of globally integrated phenomena that set Europe apart, in particular the land appropriated in the New World by Europe and the use of slave as well as other forms of unfree labor enabling the production of agricultural products and raw materials necessary for manufacturing industries. He thus explains the divergence on the basis of comparative analysis and, most importantly, the interconnections and interactions between and among regions in a global economy.

Pomeranz compares the consequences of differences in the nature of women's labor in Britain and China and shows that women's work in both countries conformed to the principles of a "market economy," which, thus, theoretically should have promoted economic growth. Although women in China worked from their homes and women in Britain were available for factory labor, if anything women's wage rates relative to men were less unequal in China than they were in Britain. But Pomeranz is not concerned with *how* gender shaped the division of labor in China and in Britain. Rather he is concerned with the fact that different cultural norms regarding gender did not economically differentiate "East" from "West."

Such global histories are important for our discussion because they highlight important considerations. First, while gender historians argue that gender is a significant factor in historical processes, this does not mean that gender is *always* critical, although it *may* be one factor among many producing a particular historical outcome. The second concerns levels of analysis. Global or even societal-level economic, social, or political trends and relations are the outcome of many complex, interacting processes. In examining or describing those outcomes, the processes contributing to them are not immediately evident. To discover them requires analysis at a more local or "micro" level and one that is concerned with process rather than structure or outcome. Let's take slavery, for example. While Europe's involvement in the slave trade and use of enslaved Africans in the New World was not by itself responsible for Western Europe's economic divergence from the rest of Eurasia in the nineteenth century, it certainly was a contributing factor. That observation is devoid of attention to gender. The work of Kathleen Brown and Kirsten Fischer discussed in Chapter 3 of this book, however, shows the significance of gender in addition to race in the establishment of slave regimes in Britain's North American colonies. But their studies work at a different level of analysis to that of Pomeranz.

A third issue raised by the recent attention to global or world history is that by emphasizing interconnections across the globe, not only is Europe displaced as the supposed motor of modern history, but history becomes something other than a story about "the nation" as a sealed, bounded, and "natural" historical home. This "trans-national" or "trans-border" approach includes what some have referred to as "the new imperial history," which has been an active concern of historians concerned with gender for some time. Examples of such scholarship will be discussed in more detail later in this chapter. But first, let us consider how feminist historians have recently explored gender in world history using primarily a comparative perspective.

In separate essays published in the same year, Alice Kessler-Harris and Laura Frader discussed gender and work or labor in world history.[26] Kessler-Harris uses several different approaches to the topic in order to suggest avenues for gender historians to follow in their effort to think globally. She explores the sexual division of labor across time and space to suggest what factors appear to be important in general in shaping the sexual division of labor, involving not only changing economic structures, but also religion and ideology, household organization, and women's and men's life-cycles. She also explores various forms of work that women have engaged and continue to engage in, including making cloth, sex work, and household labor. In addition, she suggests the impact of family organization and sexual mores on how economies were shaped and production was organized. Her contribution is to set out an agenda for future scholarship using as examples work already done on various societies across the globe and across history. Laura Frader's essay examines how the gender division of labor developed and changed over large swathes of historical time, beginning in the earliest human societies, through militarized and feudal societies across Western Europe and Asia, and the various stages of capitalist development, the industrial revolution through late twentieth-century globalization. Her survey suggests that gender divisions and inequalities have persisted over the expanse of human history. She considers possible explanations for this continuity and for the similarities in gender inequalities in different locations around the world. Such comparative histories attempt to show similarities and differences across regions or nation-states to detail the factors contributing to gender difference and how social, cultural, and economic transformations affect women and gender.

While a comparative approach is one way that some gender historians have placed their study in a global framework, a quite different kind of analysis is represented by gender historians who examine connections between and among geographically defined areas that influence gender-related knowledge, political movements, ideologies, and relationships. *Gender in World History* by Peter Stearns, published in 2000, for example, unites an approach to gender and women's history with global history understood as a study of cultural contacts and international interactions.[27] Although the naming of this approach is contested, it is generally known as "transnational" history, even if the connections being examined are not between or among "nation-states" as such. Indeed, feminist scholars concerned with empire and colonialism have led the way in moving historical analysis beyond "the nation" as a bounded and self-contained historical home. We saw examples of such research in Chapter 3 demonstrating not only that colonial rule was intrinsically bound up with issues of race, gender, and sexuality, but also that imperial culture was central to local, metropolitan (or "national") gender ideologies and politics. Such studies make contact or the connections between and among people in different geographical locations in the world central to their analyses of gender and power while at the same time recognizing that such "interconnected networks of contact and exchange" take place in contexts that shape and are shaped by "systems of power and domination."[28] Mrinalini Sinha's concept of "imperial social formation" captures the sense of interdependence between colony and metropole, envisioning them as inextricably interconnected.[29]

Sinha builds on this concept, exploring its ramifications in an analysis of the transnational debates and repercussions following the publication of Katherine Mayo's *Mother India* in 1927.[30] Very briefly, Mayo, an American feminist journalist, depicted the plight of women in India to argue against Indian nationalism and for the virtues of British rule. She blamed the condition of women on the sexual practices of Hindu men and the "backwardness" of Hindu culture more generally. The publication of the book occurred against a backdrop of US opposition to British imperialism and was intended to improve Anglo–US relations by justifying British rule of India to Americans. Its publication produced controversy across the globe. American, British, and Indian feminists, Indian nationalists and anti-imperialist groups in Britain and the United States, social reformers, politicians, and the media entered the fray. Sinha views the controversy as a global event that was both "disruptive and enabling." It entered world-wide debates about self-government and women's rights. In India itself, feminists and nationalists blamed the British for resisting social reform and doing little or nothing to improve the condition of Indian women. Indian feminists demanded that the state offer them protections rather than leaving their fate in the hands of religious communities. Thus, the controversy opened a space in which women were represented and represented themselves as citizen-subjects. Sinha's work demonstrates the potential of transnational history and the value of using approaches that link the global and the local for highlighting the changing place of gender relations and family life in Indian politics. It suggests that in the context of a global imperial social formation the media serve as a conduit for debate about gender that can affect local as well as transnational and international politics.

Research by a group of feminist historians specializing in several national or regional contexts has delved into the transnational creation via various media of a new construction of femininity in the 1920s and 1930s represented by what they term "the Modern Girl." Their research has shown that regardless of location, the images of the Modern Girl incorporated local ideas modified and transformed by "elements drawn from elsewhere."[31] The Modern Girl was not an invention of America or Europe that spread across the globe. Rather, the figure appeared to emerge nearly simultaneously through "rapidly moving and multi-directional circuits of capital, ideology and imagery."[32] Symbolizing modernity, images of the Modern Girl were featured in various advertisements for commercial products. In each of the locales where they emerged there were particular ways in which they were represented. Their social positions, ethnicities, and activities differed depending upon whether the context was Sub-Saharan Africa, South Asia, East Asia, Europe, or the United States. But across contexts they were represented as being concerned with their appearance and their bodies. Additionally, their images were bound up with ideas of skin color and race and were thus implicated in how race was understood and mobilized in various local contexts.

In an examination of the uses of the term "white men's countries" between 1890 and 1910, Marilyn Lake explores the transnational circulation of ideas about civilization and citizenship in South Africa, Canada, the United States, Australia, and New Zealand.[33] She argues that the "white

man" was a transnational figure that reflected and represented "fellow feeling" among intellectuals and political
figures in these separate nation-states connected to one
another through a transnational conversation. Using arguments about civilization and fitness for self-government that
would be repeated by other imperial powers, at the turn of
the twentieth century, the United States waged war on the
Filipinos, who were struggling for their independence. In
Australia, where the unfitness for self-government of the
Cubans and Filipinos was reiterated in the press, the declaration of the war by the United States was greeted with enthu-
siasm as several hundred men attempted to enlist at American
consulates. Lake argues that governments in South Africa,
North America, and Australasia not only identified with one
another, but looked to one another for models of racial exclusion and used similar gendered rhetoric in debates about citizenship. Furthermore, the idea of a "White Australia" was
promulgated in the context of world histories being written
in the early years of the twentieth century that saw race as a
major historical force in world civilization and political
advancement as "Australia's federal fathers drew on these
new histories and were constituted by their transnational
identification as white men under siege."[34]

It isn't just ideas that circulate through and across transnational spaces, so too do people as tourists, explorers, and,
importantly, as both voluntary and involuntary migrants.
The movement of people across geographical space certainly
is not new. People have been "on the move" from time imme-
morial. They bring with them material objects and ideas
originating in the regions from which they came and they
encounter in their new surroundings unfamiliar objects and
ways of being. In Chapter 3 we saw examples of the significance of gender and intimate relations for constituting colonial and imperial social orders. Implicit in that brief discussion
of gender, sexuality, and empire was that an imperial social
formation is constituted by the movement of people and their
interactions with others under conditions of unequal power.
In the discussion that follows we explore issues of gender
with an explicit focus on contact, mobility, and migration.

What happened to perceptions of gender difference, for
example, when explorers bent on discovering and document-

ing the lives of those in foreign lands encountered people with different cultural constructions of and expectations about gender difference? Drawing on the work of anthropologists and the journals of Captain Cook on his voyages in the Pacific in the 1760s and 1770s, Kathleen Wilson has documented what she calls the "gender misrecognition" and the "mutual" confusion that was involved in the encounter between the officers and men on the expedition and Tahitian men and women. The sailors perceived Tahitian women as sexually promiscuous, while the women, in their own eyes, were intent on exploiting boatloads of foreign men for their own advantage. The sexual activity of women in Polynesian society had a spiritual and political meaning that could not be accommodated to European ideas of morality. That Tahitian women seemed sexually brazen was unsettling to the voyagers, and accounts in their journals suggest the European men had become "the objects of Polynesian categories of difference."[35] The seamen also suspected Pacific Island men of being sodomites or effeminate. From the perspective of the men of the islands, meanwhile, for whom carrying was largely women's work, the seamen, who did such carrying themselves, might have seemed as though they were women. Another possibility that Wilson discusses is that the seamen projected their own sexual desires onto the indigenous men or that they saw in that culture an opening for them to engage in sexual acts that "back home" would be condemned.

Recent attention by historians to the movement of people across boundaries brings into view the relationship between gender and transnational, trans-border, or (to use Ballantye and Burton's term) "translocal" mobility that addresses the question of gendered subjectivities and affect in the context of global/imperial histories.[36] In Chapter 3 we learned of the "many tender ties" that cemented relationships and formed kin networks between European fur traders and native women. But as settler society moved west during the nineteenth century, intermarriage between native women and European-origin men was less tolerated. Michael A. McDonnell's fascinating account of the continuation of intimate, family ties across "racial" lines as national and linguistic borders were redrawn in the Great Lakes region of North

America after the American War of Independence suggests that in one region, at least, these ties continued to be made, not only across "racial" lines, but across the borders of Canada and the United States.[37] His study of a family history over many generations in the area known as the *pays d'en haut*, or the high country of the Great Lakes region, where Indian, French, and mixed-race or *métis* people, lived suggests that "the imagined national, cultural, and racial boundaries" did not confine its inhabitants. Rather, Indian and *métis* women continued to forge intimate ties of intermarriage and reproduction across the borders of the United States and Canada, as had their foremothers, who had crossed the imperial boundaries between the French and British empires of North America before the end of the French North American regime in 1763.

Migration across continents and oceans is an exemplar of transnationalism that long preexisted the invention of the concept. All of human history may be seen as involving people "on the move," either by their own volition in response to changing environmental or societal transformations, or involuntarily, through the fall-out of war, the slave trade, and colonialism. Historical examination of the experiences of migrants as they leave "home," attempt to establish themselves in a new environment, and maintain family ties across space reveals the centrality of gender to the various aspects of migration, emigration, and immigration. Family households, themselves, become dispersed across space and are sustained through exchanges of financial support and affection. Dirk Hoerder's global, encyclopedic analysis and survey of migration over a 1,000-year period includes a discussion of how gender inequality limited some women's ability to migrate because of their major familial responsibilities.[38] He considers how race, class, and ethnicity affected women's voluntary and forced movements, and notes how women were encouraged to move to the colonies to act as civilizing agents. Hoerder also considers their exploitation in the sex trade and as objects of contemporary sex tourism. Thus, his work suggests the various ways that gender was a central feature in one of the most important aspects of history – the movement of people across space.

Many studies of gender and migration highlight the construction of transnational family economies. Households are dispersed across space sustained by a gender division of labor that locates husbands in one locale and wives and children in another. In her studies of Italian immigration to the United States, Donna Gabaccia highlights the importance of transnational family economies sustained, on the one hand, by men who moved to the United States and South America, and, on the other, by women who remained economically active in Italy. In the nineteenth century, because of the availability of jobs for men in the receiving countries, male emigration provided a better chance of economic security for the whole family than female emigration or the emigration of the entire family.[39] Gabaccia argues more generally, that family economic considerations are primary in the decision to emigrate, regardless of the cultural background of the immigrants. In the nineteenth and early twentieth centuries, when women came to the United States they were expected to work just as they had done in the rural areas from which they came and they contributed financial support to their families of origin on the other side. This was to change later in the twentieth century when a combination of factors led women to migrate as dependants. In both the nineteenth and twentieth centuries, women's lives on both sides of the Atlantic combined waged work and domestic duties. Women's opportunities in the United States were generally limited to domestic service and labor-intensive work in the garment trades.[40]

While Gabaccia's studies focus on the gendered economic and broadly cultural factors influencing migration and the experiences of migrants, Mary Chamberlain's use of oral histories in her studies of the experiences of Caribbean immigrants in Britain opens a window onto the more affective and subjective aspects of migration. She situates her analysis of the movement of Caribbean people to and from Britain in a much longer history of movement to and from the islands – movement of people free, forced, or indentured. Transnationalism, she argues, was "built into the fabric of the Caribbean diasporic culture."[41] As people move away from and then back to the Caribbean, their families remain central. Chamberlain's work suggests that family ties across space accommodated to migration and they served to counter migration's disruptive consequences. Caribbean identity, then, was based as much on family belonging as on place of origin or location. For Chamberlain's interviewees, a transnational, dispersed family was both an economic and an emotional resource.

Both men and women migrated. Both men and women relied upon family networks for material and emotional support. But Chamberlain found that men and women talked about their migration experiences differently. While men articulated a sense that their move from the Caribbean was spontaneous and might well be temporary, women stressed the emotional distress of separation from their loved ones. In their life narratives, men articulated the sense of an independent, autonomous self using the first person, "I," to tell their story of settling in Britain. Women used the collective "we" and talked about their experiences in relation to others. Men talked about their move in terms of adventure and economic success; women stressed the emotional aspects of leaving and longing for those left behind. Thus while the circumstances of migration may have been similar for men and women, they differed in how they were explained and recounted.[42] Chamberlain's work sheds light on gendered subjectivities as they are affected by and participate in the global, transnational process of moving.

Conclusion

This chapter has surveyed and reflected upon different approaches to the study of gender history. It has reviewed the variety of ways that historians have thought about gender and history and some of the new directions of historical analysis. It also is a summary of sorts of the various issues dealt with in earlier chapters of the book: what is history and what is gender; sexuality and the body; masculinity; and the significance of gender in history. It has also reminded the reader of the emphasis throughout the book on the question of race and ethnicity, and the significance of gender and sexual relations to slavery and colonialism. By including in this last chapter examples of biographical and life history approaches and ways of reading texts to uncover subjectivities and affect, in addition to reading to ascertain the cultural construction of gender difference, and approaches that decenter both "the nation" and "the West" as motors of history, the book concludes with an appreciation of the plurality of approaches that make gender history such a vibrant field of scholarship.

Notes

Chapter 1 Why Gender History?

1   Renate Bridenthal and Claudia Koonz, "Introduction," in *Becoming Visible: Women in European History*, Boston: Houghton Mifflin, 1977: 1.
2   I will consider examples from the history of women in the United States and in Britain as representative of the kinds of questions pursued in the early years of women's history.
3   Linda Kerber, "Separate Spheres, Female Worlds, Woman's Place: The Rhetoric of Women's History," *Journal of American History* 75 (1988): 11.
4   Barbara Welter, "The Cult of True Womanhood: 1820–1860," *American Quarterly* 18 (1966): 153.
5   Carroll Smith-Rosenberg, "The Female World of Love and Ritual: Relations between Women in Nineteenth-Century America," *Signs* 1 (1975): 9.
6   Nancy F. Cott, *The Bonds of Womanhood: Women's Sphere in New England: 1780–1835*, New Haven and London: Yale University Press, 1975.
7   Sheila Rowbotham, *Woman's Consciousness, Man's World*, Harmondsworth: Penguin, 1973: 117.
8   Sheila Rowbotham, *Hidden from History: 300 Years of Women's Oppression and the Fight Against It*, London: Pluto, 1973.
9   Sally Alexander, "Women's Work in Nineteenth-Century London: A Study of the Years 1820–50," in Juliet Mitchell and

Anne Oakley, eds, *Rights and Wrongs of Women*, Harmondsworth: Penguin, 1976: 59–111.

10 Jill Liddington and Jill Norris, *One Hand Tied Behind Us: The Rise of the Women's Suffrage Movement*, London: Virago, 1978.

11 Laura Oren, "Welfare of Women in Laboring Families," *Feminist Studies* 1 (1973): 107–25.

12 Leonore Davidoff, Jean L'Esperance, and Howard Newby, "Landscape with Figures," in Juliet Mitchell and Anne Oakley, eds, *Rights and Wrongs of Women*, Harmondsworth: Penguin, 1976: 139–75.

13 Alice Kessler-Harris, "Where are the Organized Women Workers?" *Feminist Studies* 3 (1975): 92–110.

14 Alice Kessler-Harris, *Out to Work: A History of Wage-Earning Women in the United States*, New York: Oxford University Press, 1982.

15 Thomas Dublin, *Women at Work: The Transformation of Work and Community in Lowell, Massachusetts, 1826–1860*, New York: Columbia University Press, 1979.

16 Jacqueline Jones, *Labor of Love, Labor of Sorrow: Black Women, Work, and the Family from Slavery to the Present*, New York: Basic Books, 1985.

17 Christine Stansell, *City of Women: Sex and Class in New York, 1789–1860*, New York: Alfred A. Knopf, 1986.

18 London Feminist History Group, *The Sexual Dynamics of History: Men's Power, Women's Resistance*, London: Pluto, 1983: 2.

19 Ibid.: 45.

20 Joan Kelly-Gadol, "Methodological Implications of Women's History," *Signs* 4 (1976): 809–23.

21 Natalie Zemon Davis, "Women's History in Transition," *Feminist Studies* 3 (1976): 90.

22 Judith L. Newton, Mary P. Ryan, and Judith R. Walkowitz, "Editors' Introduction," in *Sex and Class in Women's History*, London: Routledge, 1983: 1.

23 Ibid.

24 Renate Bridenthal, Claudia Koonz, and Susan Stuard, "Introduction," in *Becoming Visible: Women in European History*, 2nd edition, Boston: Houghton Mifflin, 1987: 1.

25 Joan Wallach Scott, "Gender: A Useful Category of Historical Analysis," in *Gender and the Politics of History*, revised edition, New York: Columbia University Press, 1999: 28–50, esp. 28–31.

26 Joan Wallach Scott, "Introduction," in ibid.: 6.

27   Mrinalini Sinha, *Colonial Masculinity. The "Manly English-man" and the "Effeminate Bengali" in the Late Nineteenth Century*, Manchester: Manchester University Press, 1995.

28   Joan Hoff, "Gender as a Postmodern Category of Paralysis," *Women's History Review* 3 (1994): 149.

29   Ibid.: 159.

30   June Purvis, "From 'Women Worthies' to Poststructuralism? Debate and Controversy in Women's History in Britain," in June Purvis, ed., *Women's History in Britain, 1850–1945: An Introduction*, London: UCL Press, 1995: 13.

31   For a vigorous defense of the usefulness of the term "patriar-chy," see Judith Bennett, "Feminism and History," *Gender & History* 1 (1989): 251–72.

32   Nancy F. Cott and Drew Gilpin Faust, "Recent Directions in Gender and Women's History," *OAH Magazine of History* 19 (2005): 4–5.

33   The editors, "Why Gender and History?" *Gender & History* 1 (1989): 1–2.

34   Michele Riot-Sarcey, "The Difficulties of Gender in France: Reflections on a Concept," in Leonore Davidoff, Keith McClelland, and Eleni Varikas, *Gender and History: Retrospect and Prospect*, Oxford: Blackwell, 2000: 71–80.

35   Gail Hershatter and Wang Zheng, "Chinese History: A Useful Category of Gender Analysis," *American Historical Review* 113 (2008): 1404–21, esp. pp. 1412–21.

Chapter 2   Bodies and Sexuality in Gender History

1   Joan Wallach Scott, *Gender and the Politics of History*, revised edition, New York: Columbia University, 1999: ix–xiii and 197–222.

2   Mary P. Ryan, *The Mysteries of Sex: Tracing Women and Men through American History*, Chapel Hill: University of North Carolina Press, 2006.

3   Londa Schiebinger, *Nature's Body: Gender in the Making of Modern Science*, Boston: Beacon, 1993.

4   Thomas Laqueur, *Making Sex: Body and Gender from the Greeks to Freud*, Cambridge, MA: Harvard University Press, 1990.

5   Schiebinger, *Nature's Body*: 122.

6   For critiques see: Katharine Park and Robert A. Nye, "Destiny is Anatomy," *New Republic*, February 18, 1991: 53–7; Michael Stolberg, "A Woman Down to Her Bones: The Anatomy of Sexual Difference in the Sixteenth and Early Seventeenth Cen-

turies," *Isis* 94 (2003): 274–99; and Dror Wahrman, "Change and the Corporeal in Seventeenth- and Eighteenth-Century Gender History: Or, Can Cultural History Be Rigorous?" *Gender & History* 20 (2008): 584–602.

7   See Judith Butler, *Gender Trouble*, London: Routledge, 1990; *Bodies that Matter: On the Discursive Limits of "Sex,"* London: Routledge, 1993.

8   Raewyn Connell, *Gender and Power*, Cambridge: Polity, 1987: 87.

9   Ibid.: 84.

10   Elizabeth Grosz, *Volatile Bodies: Toward a Corporeal Feminism*, Bloomington: Indiana University Press, 1994; Anne Fausto-Sterling, *Sexing the Body: Gender Politics and the Construction of Sexuality*, New York: Basic Books, 2000.

11   Kathleen Canning, "The Body as Method?" in her *Gender History in Practice: Historical Perspectives on Bodies, Class, and Citizenship*, Ithaca: Cornell University Press, 2006.

12   Joanna Bourke, *Dismembering the Male: Men's Bodies, Britain and the Great War*, London: Reaktion Books, 1996.

13   See, especially, Mary Poovey, *Making a Social Body: British Cultural Formation, 1830–1864*, Chicago: University of Chicago Press, 1995.

14   Caroline Walker Bynum, *Holy Feast and Holy Fast: The Religious Significance of Food to Medieval Women*, Berkeley and Los Angeles: University of California Press, 1988.

15   Dorinda Outram, *The Body and the French Revolution: Sex, Class, and Political Culture*, New Haven: Yale University Press, 1989.

16   Lynn Hunt, "Freedom of Dress in Revolutionary France," in Londa Schiebinger, ed., *Feminism and the Body*, Oxford: Oxford University Press, 2000: 182–202.

17   Isabel V. Hull, *Sexuality, State and Civil Society in Germany, 1700–1815*, Ithaca: Cornell University Press, 1996: 225.

18   Douglas Northrop, *Veiled Empire: Gender and Power in Stalinist Central Asia*, Ithaca: Cornell University Press, 2004.

19   Joan Wallach Scott, *Politics of the Veil*, Princeton: Princeton University Press, 2007.

20   Afsaneh Najmabadi, *Women with Mustaches and Men without Beards: Gender and Sexual Anxieties of Iranian Modernity*, Berkeley: University of California Press, 2005.

21   Raewyn Connell, "Sexual Revolution," in Lynne Segal, ed., *New Sexual Agendas*, Basingstoke: Macmillan, 1997: 70.

22   Michel Foucault, *The History of Sexuality, Vol. 1: An Introduction*, London: Allen Lane, 1979.

23 Jeffrey Weeks, *Sexuality*, 2nd edition. London: Routledge, 2003: 30. Emphasis added.

24 David Halperin, *One Hundred Years of Homosexuality and Other Essays on Greek Love*, London: Routledge, 1990.

25 For an overview see Leila J. Rupp, "Toward a Global History of Same-Sex Sexuality," *Journal of the History of Sexuality* 10 (2001): 287–302.

26 Helmut Puff, *Sodomy in Reformation Germany and Switzerland 1400–1600*, Chicago: University of Chicago Press, 2003.

27 Robert A. Nye, "Sexuality," in Teresa A. Meade and Merry E. Wiesner-Hanks, eds, *A Companion to Gender History*, Oxford: Blackwell, 2006: 15.

28 Randolph Trumbach, *Sex and the Gender Revolution, Vol. I: Heterosexuality and the Third Gender in Enlightenment London*, Chicago: University of Chicago Press, 1998.

29 George Chauncey, *Gay New York: Gender, Urban Culture and the Makings of the Gay Male World 1890–1940*, New York: Basic Books, 1994.

30 Martha Vicinus, "Introduction" to Martha Vicinus, ed., *Lesbian Subjects: A Feminist Studies Reader*, Bloomington: Indiana University Press, 1996: 2–3.

31 Ibid.: 8–9.

32 Martha Vicinus, *Intimate Friends: Women Who Loved Women, 1778–1928*, Chicago: University of Chicago Press, 2004.

33 Elizabeth Lapovsky Kennedy and Madeline D. Davis, *Boots of Leather, Slippers of Gold: The History of a Lesbian Community*, New York: Routledge, 1993.

34 Hull, *Sexuality*.

35 Ruth Mazo Karras, *Common Women: Prostitution and Sexuality in Medieval England*, Oxford: Oxford University Press, 1996: 140.

36 Lyndal Roper, *The Holy Household: Women and Morals in Reformation Augsburg*, Oxford: Oxford University Press, 1989: 129.

37 Judith Walkowitz, *Prostitution and Victorian Society: Women, Class and the State*, Cambridge: Cambridge University Press, 1980.

38 Philippa Levine, *Prostitution, Race and Politics: Policing Venereal Disease in the British Empire*, London: Routledge, 2003.

39 Annette F. Timm, "Sex with a Purpose: Prostitution, Venereal Disease, and Militarized Masculinity in the Third Reich," *Journal of the History of Sexuality* 11 (2002): 223–55.

Chapter 3 Gender and Other Relations of Difference

1 Vicki L. Ruiz and Ellen Carol DuBois, eds, *Unequal Sisters: A Multicultural Reader in US Women's History*, 3rd edition, London: Routledge, 2000: xi. Internal quotes attributed to Joanne Meyerowitz.
2 Ibid.: xiii.
3 Gisela Bock, "Women's History and Gender History: Aspects of an International Debate," *Gender & History* 1 (1989): 15, 20.
4 Linda Gordon, "Black and White Visions of Welfare: Women's Welfare Activism," in Ruiz and DuBois, eds, *Unequal Sisters*: 214–41.
5 Nancy Hewitt, " 'Charity or Mutual Aid?': Two Perspectives on Latin Women's Philanthropy in Tampa, Florida," in Kathleen D. McCarthy, ed., *Lady Bountiful Revisited: Women, Philanthropy and Power*, New Brunswick, NJ: Rutgers University Press, 1990: 55–69.
6 Ellen Ross, *Love and Toil: Motherhood in Outcast London, 1870–1918*, Oxford: Oxford University Press, 1993: 204.
7 Gwendolyn Mink, *Wages of Motherhood*, Ithaca: Cornell University Press, 1995: see esp. Chapter 1.
8 Nayan Shah, "Cleansing Motherhood: Hygiene and the Culture of Domesticity in San Francisco's Chinatown, 1875–1900," in Antoinette Burton, ed., *Gender, Sexuality and Colonial Modernities*, London: Routledge, 1999: 19–32.
9 Clare Midgley, *Women against Slavery: The British Campaigns, 1780–1870*, London: Routledge, 1992: 200.
10 Catherine Hall, *Civilising Subjects: Metropole and Colony in the English Imagination 1830–1867*, Chicago: University of Chicago Press, 2002: 95.
11 Ibid.: 97.
12 Antoinette Burton, *Burdens of History: British Feminists, Indian Women and Imperial Culture 1865–1955*, Chapel Hill: University of North Carolina Press, 1994.
13 Melanie Newton, "Philanthropy, Gender, and the Production of Public Life in Barbados, ca 1790–ca 1850," in Pamela Scully and Diana Paton, eds, *Gender and Slave Emancipation in the Atlantic World*, Durham, NC: Duke University Press, 2005: 225–46.
14 Hall, *Civilising Subjects*: 16.
15 Deborah Gray White, *Ar'n't I a Woman?: Female Slaves in the Plantation South*, New York: W. W. Norton, 1985.

16   Jacqueline Jones, *Labor of Love, Labor of Sorrow: Black Women, Work, and the Family, from Slavery to the Present*, New York: Vintage, 1985.

17   Kathleen M. Brown, *Good Wives, Nasty Wenches and Anxious Patriarchs: Gender, Race and Power in Colonial Virginia*, Chapel Hill: University of North Carolina Press, 1996: 4.

18   Ibid.

19   Ibid.: 104.

20   Ibid.: 2.

21   Hilary McD. Beckles, "Freeing Slavery: Gender Paradigms in the Social History of Caribbean Slavery," in Brian L. Moore, B. W. Higman, Carl Campbell, and Patrick Bryan, eds, *Slavery, Freedom and Gender*, Barbados: University of the West Indies Press, 2001: 197–231.

22   Jennifer L. Morgan, *Laboring Women: Reproduction and Gender in New World Slavery*, Philadelphia: University of Pennsylvania Press, 2004.

23   Kirsten Fischer, *Suspect Relations: Sex, Race, and Resistance in Colonial North Carolina*, Ithaca: Cornell University Press, 2002: 11.

24   Pamela Scully, "Rape, Race, and Colonial Culture: The Sexual Politics of Identity in the Nineteenth-Century Cape Colony, South Africa," *American Historical Review* 100 (1995): 388.

25   The term "imperial social formation" was coined by Mrinalini Sinha, *Colonial Masculinity: The "Manly Englishman" and the "Effeminate Bengali" in the Late Nineteenth Century*, Manchester: Manchester University Press, 1995: 2.

26   Philippa Levine, "Sexuality, Gender and Empire," in Philippa Levine, ed., *Gender and Empire*, Oxford: Oxford University Press, 2004: 134.

27   Ann Laura Stoler, "Making Empire Respectable: The Politics of Race and Sexual Morality in 20th-Century Colonial Cultures," *American Ethnologist* 16 (1989): 637.

28   Levine, "Sexuality": 137.

29   Mary A. Procida, *Married to the Empire: Gender, Politics and Imperialism in India, 1883–1947*, Manchester: Manchester University Press, 2002.

30   Stoler, "Making Empire": 641.

31   Adele Perry, *On the Edge of Empire: Gender, Race, and the Making of British Columbia, 1849–1871*, Toronto: University of Toronto Press, 2001.

32   Sylvia Van Kirk, *"Many Tender Ties": Women in Fur-Trade Society in Western Canada, 1670–1870*, Winnipeg, Manitoba: Watson and Dwyer, 1981.

33 Sylvia Van Kirk, "From 'Marrying-In' to 'Marrying-Out': Changing Patterns of Aboriginal/Non-Aboriginal Marriage in Colonial Canada," *Frontiers* 23 (2002): 1–11.

34 See Ann Laura Stoler, "Sexual Affronts and Racial Frontiers: European Identities and the Cultural Politics of Exclusion in Colonial Southeast Asia," *Comparative Studies in Society and History* 34 (1992): 514–51. See also the essays in Ann Laura Stoler, ed., *Haunted by Empire: Geographies of Intimacy in North American History*, Durham, NC: Duke University Press, 2006.

35 Tyler Stovall, "Love, Labor and Race: Colonial Men and White Women in France during the Great War," in Tyler Stovall and Georges Van Den Abbeele, eds, *French Civilization and Its Discontents: Nationalism, Colonialism and Race*, Lanham, MD: Lexington Books, 2003: 307.

36 Ibid.: 313.

Chapter 4   Men and Masculinity

1 Michael S. Kimmel, *The History of Men: Essays in the History of American and British Masculinities*, Albany: SUNY Press, 2005: ix.

2 Gail Bederman, *Manliness and Civilization: A Cultural History of Gender and Race in the United States, 1880–1917*, Chicago: University of Chicago Press, 1996: 18.

3 Christopher E. Forth and Bertrand Taithe, "Introduction," in Forth and Taithe, eds, *French Masculinities: History, Culture, Politics*, Basingstoke: Palgrave Macmillan, 2007: 6.

4 See John Tosh, "What Should Historians Do with Masculinity? Reflections on Nineteenth-Century Britain," *History Workshop Journal* 38 (1994): 179–201.

5 Judith Kegan Gardiner, "Introduction," in Gardiner, ed., *Masculinity Studies and Feminist Theory: New Directions*, New York: Columbia University Press, 2002: 11.

6 Tosh, "What Should Historians Do?": 183.

7 Stefan Dudink, "Masculinity, Effeminacy, Time: Conceptual Change in the Dutch Age of Democratic Revolutions," in Stefan Dudink, Karen Hagemann, and John Tosh, eds, *Masculinities in Politics and War: Gendering Modern History*, Manchester: Manchester University Press, 2004: 78.

8 David Gilmore, *Manhood in the Making: Cultural Concepts of Masculinity*, New Haven: Yale University Press, 1990: 17.

9 Forth and Taithe, "Introduction": 4.
10 Ruth Mazo Karras, *From Boys to Men: Formations of Masculinity in Late Medieval Europe*, Philadelphia: University of Pennsylvania Press, 2003: 11.
11 Ibid.: 67.
12 Ibid.: 109.
13 Alexandra Shepard, *Meanings of Manhood in Early Modern England*, Oxford: Oxford University Press, 2003: 3.
14 Ibid.: 96.
15 Ibid.
16 Ibid.: 248.
17 Kathleen M. Brown, *Good Wives, Nasty Wenches and Anxious Patriarchs: Gender, Race and Power in Colonial Virginia*, Chapel Hill: University of North Carolina Press, 1996, esp.: 138–40.
18 Ibid.: 139.
19 Ibid.: 140.
20 Ibid.: 185.
21 Ibid.: 366.
22 Anne S. Lombard, *Making Manhood. Growing Up Male in Colonial New England*, Cambridge, MA: Harvard University Press, 2003: 9.
23 Ibid.: 12.
24 Ibid.: 72.
25 Robert A. Nye, *Masculinity and Male Codes of Honor in Modern France*, Oxford: Oxford University Press, 1993: 167.
26 Ibid.: 71.
27 Ibid.: 13.
28 Christopher E. Forth, *The Dreyfus Affair and the Crisis of French Manhood*, Baltimore and London: Johns Hopkins University Press, 2004: 62.
29 Ibid.: 171.
30 Angus McLaren, *The Trials of Masculinity: Policing Sexual Boundaries 1870–1930*, Chicago: University of Chicago Press, 1997: 35.
31 Bederman, *Manliness and Civilization*: 44.
32 Michael S. Kimmel, "After Fifteen Years: The Impact of the Sociology of Masculinity on the Masculinity of Sociology," in Jeff Hearn and David Morgan, eds, *Men, Masculinities and Social Theory*, London: Unwin Hyman, 1990: 100.
33 Lynne Segal, *Slow Motion: Changing Masculinities, Changing Men*, 3rd revised edition, Basingstoke, Palgrave, 2007: xxiv.
34 Amy S. Greenberg, *Manifest Manhood and the Antebellum American Empire*, Cambridge: Cambridge University Press, 2005: 8.

35 Ibid.: 12.
36 Ibid.: 272, 273.
37 Kristin L. Hoganson, *Fighting for American Manhood: How Gender Politics Provoked the Spanish–American and Philippine–American Wars*, New Haven: Yale University Press, 1998: 201.
38 Ibid.: 14.
39 Ibid.: 202.
40 Ibid.: 96.
41 Mrinalini Sinha, *Colonial Masculinity. The "Manly Englishman" and the "Effeminate Bengali" in the Late Nineteenth Century*, Manchester: Manchester University Press, 1995.
42 Ibid.: 4.
43 Ibid.: 41.
44 Heather Streets, *Martial Races: The Military, Race, and Masculinity in British Imperial Culture, 1857–1914*, Manchester: Manchester University Press, 2004.
45 Ibid.: 11.
46 Ibid.: 157.
47 Ibid.: 133.
48 Ibid.: 139–40.
49 Ibid.: 225.
50 As quoted in Bederman, *Manliness*: 2.
51 Ibid.
52 Patrick McDevitt, *May the Best Man Win: Sport, Masculinity, and Nationalism in Great Britain and the Empire, 1880–1935*, Basingstoke: Palgrave, 2004: 58–80.
53 Ibid.: 71.
54 As quoted in ibid.: 78.
55 Ibid.: 79.
56 Ibid.: 80.
57 Leonore Davidoff and Catherine Hall, *Family Fortunes: Men and Women of the English Middle Class, 1780–1850*, revised edition, London: Routledge, 2002: 227.
58 Ibid.: 329.
59 Ibid.: 335.
60 John Tosh, *A Man's Place: Masculinity and the Middle-Class Home in Victorian England*, New Haven and London: Yale University Press, 1999: 4.
61 Ibid.: 6.
62 Ibid.: 7.
63 Ibid.: 189.
64 Ibid.: 194.
65 Martin Francis, "The Domestication of the Male? Recent Research on Nineteenth- and Twentieth-Century British Masculinity," *The Historical Journal* 45 (2002): 641.

66   Martin Francis, *The Flyer: British Culture and the Royal Air Force 1939–1945*, Oxford: Oxford University Press, 2008: 84.

67   David B. Marshall, " 'A Canoe, and a Tent and God's Great Out-of-Doors': Muscular Christianity and the Flight from Domesticity, 1880s–1930s," in Heather E. Ellis and Jessica M. Meyer, eds, *Masculinity and the Other: Historical Perspectives*, Newcastle: Cambridge Scholars, 2009: 25–39.

68   Michael Roper, "Maternal Relations: Moral Manliness and Emotional Survival in Letters Home during the First World War," in Stefan Dudink, Karen Hagemann, and John Tosh, eds, *Masculinities in Politics and War: Gendering Modern History*, Manchester: Manchester University Press, 2004: 295–316.

69   Ibid.: 311.

70   Mrinalini Sinha, "Giving Masculinity a History: Some Contributions from the Historiography of Colonial India," in Leonore Davidoff, Keith McClelland, and Eleni Varikas, eds, *Gender and History: Retrospect and Prospect*. Oxford: Blackwell, 2000: esp. 35–7.

Chapter 5   Gender and Historical Knowledge

1   Ann M. Little, *Abraham in Arms: War and Gender in Colonial New England*, Philadelphia: University of Pennsylvania Press, 2007: 3.

2   Ibid.: 7.

3   Ibid.: 9.

4   As quoted in Linda K. Kerber, " 'History Can Do It No Justice': Women and the Reinterpretation of the American Revolution," in Ronald Hoffman and Peter J. Albert, eds, *Women in the Age of the American Revolution*, Charlottesville: University of Virginia Press, 1989: 3–42.

5   Mary Beth Norton, *Liberty's Daughters: The Revolutionary Experience of American Women, 1750–1800*, Ithaca: Cornell University Press, 1996: 298–9.

6   Ruth H. Bloch, "The Construction of Gender in a Republican World," in Jack P. Greene and J. R. Pole, eds, *A Companion to the American Revolution*, Oxford: Blackwell, 2000: 606.

7   Ibid.: 607.

8   Mary P. Ryan, *Mysteries of Sex: Tracing Women and Men through American History*, Chapel Hill: University of North Carolina Press, 2006: 154.

9 Susan Juster, *Disorderly Women: Sexual Politics and Evangelicalism in Revolutionary New England*, Ithaca: Cornell University Press, 1994.

10 Ibid.: 216.

11 Lynn Hunt, "The Many Bodies of Marie Antoinette: Political Pornography and the Problem of the Feminine in the French Revolution," in Gary Kates, ed., *The French Revolution: Recent Debates and New Controversies*, 2nd edition, New York: Routledge, 1998: 203.

12 Ibid.: 206.

13 As quoted in "Sunshine for Women," http://www.pinn.net/~sunshine/book-sum/gouges.html.

14 Lynn Hunt, *Family Romance of the French Revolution*, Berkeley: University of California Press, 1992: 82.

15 Ibid.: 154.

16 Suzanne Desan, *The Family on Trial in Revolutionary France*, Berkeley: University of California Press, 2004: 90.

17 Benedict Anderson, *Imagined Communities: Reflections on the Origin and Spread of Nationalism*, revised edition, London: Verso, 1991.

18 Ernest Gellner, *Nations and Nationalism*, Oxford: Blackwell, 1983: 6.

19 Anne McClintock, " 'No Longer in a Future Heaven'": Nationalism, Gender, and Race," in Geoff Eley and Ronald Grigor Suny, eds, *Becoming National*, Oxford: Oxford University Press, 1996: 260.

20 Julie Skurski, "The Ambiguities of Authenticity in Latin America: Dona Barbara and the Construction of National Identity," in Geoff Eley and Ronald Grigor Suny, eds, *Becoming National*, Oxford: Oxford University Press, 1996: 371–402.

21 This discussion and some of what follows draws from Mrinalini Sinha, *Gender and Nation*, Washington, DC: The American Historical Association, 2006.

22 Joan B. Landes, *Visualizing the Nation: Gender, Representation, and Revolution in Eighteenth-Century France*, Ithaca: Cornell University Press, 2001: 136.

23 Quoted in Joan B. Landes, "Republican Citizenship and Heterosocial Desire: Concepts of Masculinity in Revolutionary France," in Stefan Dudink, Karen Hagemann, and John Tosh, eds, *Masculinities in Politics and War: Gendering Modern History*, Manchester: Manchester University Press, 2004: 97.

24 Asfenah Najmabadi, *Women with Mustaches and Men without Beards: Gender and Sexual Anxieties of Iranian Modernity*, Berkeley: University of California Press, 2005: 116.

25   Lisa Pollard, *Nurturing the Nation: The Family Politics of Modernizing, Colonizing, and Liberating Egypt*, Berkeley: University of California Press, 2005: 8.
26   Ibid.: 10.
27   Ibid.: 196.
28   Beth Baron, *Egypt as a Woman: Nationalism, Gender, and Politics*, Berkeley: University of California Press, 2005: 55.
29   This discussion is based on Kumari Jayawardena, *Feminism and Nationalism in the Third World*, London: Zed Books, 1986: 25–56.
30   Susan L. Glosser, *Chinese Visions of Family and State, 1915–1950*, Berkeley: University of California Press, 2003: 4.
31   Christina Kelley Gilmartin, *Engendering the Chinese Revolution: Radical Women, Communist Politics, and Mass Movements in the 1920s*, Berkeley: University of California Press, 1995: 19.
32   Stefan Dudink and Karen Hagemann, "Masculinity in Politics and War in the Age of Democratic Revolutions, 1750–1850," in Stefan Dudink, Karen Hagemann, and John Tosh, eds, *Masculinities in Politics and War: Gendering Modern History*, Manchester: Manchester University Press, 2004: 7.
33   Ibid.: 11.
34   Michael J. Hughes, "Making Frenchmen into Warriors: Martial Masculinity in Napoleonic France," in Christopher E. Forth and Bertrand Taithe, *French Masculinities: History, Culture and Politics*, Houndmills, Basingstoke: Palgrave, 2007: 31–63.
35   Karen Hagemann, " 'Heroic Virgins' and 'Bellicose Amazons': Armed Women, the Gender Order, and the German Public during and after the Anti-Napoleonic Wars," *European History Quarterly* 37 (2007): 507–27.
36   For a thorough analysis of the term "total war" and the origins of the term "home front," see Karen Hagemann, "Home/Front: The Military, Violence and Gender Relations in the Age of the World Wars," in Karen Hagemann and Stefanie-Schuler-Springorum, eds, *Home/Front: The Military, War and Gender in Twentieth-Century Germany*, Oxford: Berg, 2002: 1–41.
37   Nicoletta F. Gullace, *"The Blood of Our Sons": Men, Women, and the Renegotiation of British Citizenship during the Great War*, Houndsmills, Basingstoke: Palgrave Macmillan, 2002: 182.
38   Matthew McCormack, *The Independent Man: Citizenship and Gender Politics in Georgian England*, Manchester: Manchester University Press, 2005: 52.

39 Ibid.: 133.
40 Ibid.: 197.
41 Anna Clark, *The Struggle for the Breeches: Gender and the Making of the British Working Class*, Berkeley: University of California Press, 1995.
42 This discussion is based on Catherine Hall, "The Rule of Difference: Gender, Class and Empire in the Making of the 1832 Reform Act," in Ida Blom, Karen Hagemann, and Catherine Hall, eds, *Gendered Nations: Nationalisms and Gender Order in the Long Nineteenth Century*, Oxford: Berg, 2000: 107–35.
43 Keith McClelland, "England's Greatness, the Working Man," in Catherine Hall, Keith McClelland, and Jane Rendall, *Defining the Victorian Nation: Class, Race, Gender and the British Reform Act of 1867*, Cambridge: Cambridge University Press, 2000: 101.
44 Ibid.: 71.

Chapter 6   Assessing "Turns" and New Directions

1 Geoff Eley and Keith Nield, *The Future of Class in History: What's Left of the Social?* Ann Arbor: University of Michigan Press, 2007: 68.
2 Kathleen Canning, *Gender History in Practice: Historical Perspectives on Bodies, Class, and Citizenship*, Ithaca: Cornell University Press, 2006: 63–100.
3 Bryan Palmer, *Descent into Discourse*, Philadelphia: Temple University Press, 1990: 186.
4 For a discussion see Lisa Duggan, "The Theory Wars, or, Who's Afraid of Judith Butler?" *Journal of Women's History* 10 (1998): 9–20.
5 Joan Wallach Scott, "Gender: A Useful Category of Historical Analysis," in *Gender and the Politics of History*, revised edition, New York: Columbia University Press, 1999: 28–50.
6 Judith Walkowitz, *City of Dreadful Delight: Narratives of Sexual Danger in Late-Victorian London*, London: Virago, 1992.
7 Canning, *Gender History*: 87.
8 Ibid.: 97.
9 Ibid.
10 Peter Burke, *What is Cultural History?* Cambridge: Polity Press, 2004: Chapters 4 and 5.
11 Eley and Nield, *The Future of Class*: 194.
12 Canning, *Gender History*: 212–37.

13   Michael Roper, "Slipping Out of View: Subjectivity and Emotion in Gender History," *History Workshop Journal* 59 (2005): 57–72.
14   Ibid.: 60.
15   Ibid.: 62.
16   Ibid.: 65.
17   Ibid.: 69.
18   Timothy G. Ashplant, *Fractured Loyalties: Masculinity, Class and Politics in Britain, 1900–30*, London: Rivers Oram, 2007: 4.
19   Ibid.: 18.
20   Ibid.: 10–11.
21   Ibid.: 11.
22   Lyndal Roper, *Oedipus and the Devil: Witchcraft, Sexuality and Religion in Early Modern Europe*, London: Routledge, 1994: 228.
23   Ibid.: 17.
24   For a discussion of the issue of "scale," see Antoinette Burton, "Not Even Remotely Global? Method and Scale in World History," *History Workshop Journal* 64 (2007): 323–8.
25   Kenneth Pomeranz, *The Great Divergence: China, Europe, and the Making of the Modern World Economy*, Princeton: Princeton University Press, 2000.
26   Alice Kessler-Harris, "Gender and Work: Possibilities for a Global Historical Overview," in Bonnie G. Smith, ed., *Women's History in Global Perspective*, Urbana: University of Illinois Press, 2004: 145–94; Laura Frader, "Gender and Labor in World History," in Teresa A. Meade and Merry E. Wiesner-Hanks, eds, *A Companion to Gender History*, Oxford: Blackwell, 2004: 26–50.
27   Peter N. Stearns, *Gender in World History*, London: Routledge, 2000.
28   Tony Ballantye and Antoinette Burton, "Introduction," in Ballantye and Burton, eds, *Bodies in Contact: Rethinking Colonial Encounters in World History*, Durham, NC: Duke University Press, 2005: 3.
29   Mrinalini Sinha, "Mapping an Imperial Social Formation: A Modest Proposal for Feminist Historiography," *Signs* 25 (2000): 1077–82.
30   Mrinalini Sinha, *Specters of Mother India: The Global Restructuring of an Empire*, Durham, NC: Duke University Press, 2006.
31   Tani E. Barlow, Madeleine Yue Dong, Uta G. Poiger, Priti Ramamurthy, Lynn M. Thomas, and Alys Eve Weinbaum,

"The Modern Girl around the World: A Research Agenda and Preliminary Findings," *Gender & History* 17 (2005): 246.

32 Ibid.: 248.

33 Marilyn Lake, "Fellow Feeling: A Transnational Perspective on Conceptions of Civil Society and Citizenship in 'White Men's Countries' 1890–1910," in Karen Hagemann, Sonya Michel, and Gunilla Budde, eds, *Civil Society and Gender Justice: Historical and Comparative Perspectives*, Oxford: Berghahn Books, 2008: 265–84.

34 Marilyn Lake, "The White Man under Siege: New Histories of Race in the Nineteenth Century and the Advent of White Australia," *History Workshop Journal* 58 (2004): 58.

35 Kathleen Wilson, "Thinking Back: Gender Misrecognition and Polynesian Subversions aboard the Cook Voyages," in Kathleen Wilson, ed., *A New Imperial History: Culture, Identity and Modernity in Britain and the Empire 1660–1840*, Cambridge: Cambridge University Press, 2004: 352.

36 Tony Ballantyne and Antoinette Burton, eds, *Moving Subjects: Gender, Mobility, and Intimacy in an Age of Global Empire*, Urbana: University of Illinois Press, 2009, "Introduction," 9, and "Epilogue: The Intimate, the Translocal, and the Imperial in an Age of Mobility," 335–8.

37 Michael A. McDonnell, " '*Il a Épousé une Sauvagesse*': Indian and *Métis* Persistence across Imperial and National Borders," in Tony Ballantye and Antoinette Burton, eds, *Moving Subjects: Gender, Mobility, and Intimacy in an Age of Global Empire*, Urbana: University of Illinois Press, 2009: 149–71.

38 Dirk Hoerder, *Cultures in Contact: World Migration in the Second Millennium*, Durham, NC: Duke University Press, 2002.

39 Donna Gabaccia, "When the Migrants are Men: Italy's Women and Transnationalism as a Working-Class Way of Life," in Pamela Sharpe, ed., *Women, Gender and Labour Migration: Historical and Global Perspectives*, London: Routledge, 2001.

40 Donna Gabaccia, *From the Other Side: Women, Gender, and Immigrant life in the US, 1820–1990*, Bloomington: Indiana University Press, 1994.

41 Mary Chamberlain, *Family Love in the Diaspora*, New Brunswick, NJ: Transaction Publishers, 2006: 94.

42 Mary Chamberlain, *Narratives of Exile and Return*, London: St Martin's Press, 1997; reissued London: Transaction Publishers, 2005.

Suggestions for Further Reading

The list of suggestions for further reading is not meant to be comprehensive. It will necessarily be selective and it is not meant to be definitive. The categories in which the suggestions are placed are not mutually exclusive. Several of the suggestions fit into more than one grouping. Also, in the main, I have listed relatively recent works rather than older "classics" so that readers can become further acquainted with reasonably up-to-date scholarship in the field. Generally, I have not included titles discussed in the course of this book and those cited in the endnotes, with the exception of edited collections. But the reader is strongly encouraged to include these works as suggestions for further reading as many of them would be included in a comprehensive list of significant contributions to the study of gender history.

Chapter 1 Why Gender History?

For overviews of the field and helpful collections of essays on the broad topic of gender in history, see S. Brownell and J. Wasserstrom, eds, *Chinese Feminities/Chinese Masculinities: A Reader* (Berkeley: University of California Press, 2002); R. Connell, *Gender in World Perspective* (Cambridge: Polity, 2009); L. Davidoff, K. McClelland, and E. Varikas, eds,

Gender and History: Retrospect and Prospect (Oxford: Blackwell, 2000); L. Downs, *Writing Gender History*, 2nd edition (London: Hodder Arnold, 2009); D. Glover and C. Kaplan, *Genders*, 2nd edition (New York: Routledge, 2009); S. Kent, *Gender and Power in Britain 1640–1990* (London: Routledge, 1999); L. Kerber, A. Kessler-Harris, and K. Sklar, eds, *Women and History: New Feminist Essays* (Chapel Hill: University of North Carolina Press, 1995); S. Kleinberg, E. Boris, and V. Ruiz, eds, *The Practice of US Women's History: Narratives, Intersections and Dialogues* (New Brunswick, NJ: Rutgers University Press, 2007); T. Meade and M. Wiesner-Hanks, eds, *A Companion to Gender History* (Oxford: Blackwell, 2004); J. Parr, "Gender History and Historical Practice," *Canadian Historical* Review 76 (1995): 354–76; V. Ruiz with E. C. DuBois, eds, *Unequal Sisters: An Inclusive Reader in US Women's History*, 4th edition (London: Routledge, 2008); M. Wiesner-Hanks, *Gender in History: New Perspectives on the Past* (Malden, MA: Blackwell, 2001); M. Wiesner-Hanks, *Women and Gender in Early Modern Europe*, 3rd edition (Cambridge: Cambridge University Press, 2008). For two books of essays that comment on "history," see J. M. Bennett, *History Matters: Patriarchy and the Challenge of Feminism* (Manchester: Manchester University Press, 2006) and B. G. Smith, *The Gender of History: Men, Women and Historical Practice* (Cambridge, MA: Harvard University Press, 1998).

Chapter 2   Bodies and Sexuality in Gender History

For insightful essays on the sex/gender distinction, see R. Braidotti, "The Uses and Abuses of the Sex Distinction in European Feminist Practices," in G. Griffin and R. Braidotti, eds, *Thinking Differently: A Reader in European Women's Studies* (London: Zed Books, 2002) and A. Najmabadi, "Beyond the Americas: Are Gender and Sexuality Useful Categories of Historical Analysis?" *Journal of Women's History* 18 (2006): 11–21. On science and sex/gender, L. Jordanova, *Nature Displayed: Gender, Science and Medicine*

1760–1820 (London: Longman, 1999); N. Stepan, "Race, Gender, Science and Citizenship," *Gender & History* 10 (1998): 25–52. On the body, see C. Bynum, "Why All the Fuss about the Body? A Medievalist's Perspective," *Critical Inquiry* 22 (1995): 1–33; L. Frader, "From Muscles to Nerves: Gender, 'Race', and the Body at Work in France, 1919–1939," *International Review of Social History* 44 (1999), supplement: 123–47; D. Smail, *On Deep History and the Brain* (Berkeley: University of California Press, 2008). On sexuality, see L. Bland, "White Women and Men of Colour: Miscegenation Fears in Britain after the Great War," *Gender & History* 17 (2005): 29–61; J. Bristow, *Sexuality* (London: Routledge, 1997); M. Cook, R. Mills, R. Trumbach, and H. Cocks, *A Gay History of Britain: Love and Sex between Men since the Middle Ages* (Oxford: Greenwood World, 2007); J. D'Emilio and E. B. Freedman, *Intimate Matters: A History of Sexuality in America*, 2nd edition (Chicago: University of Chicago Press, 1997); M. Houlbrook, *Queer London: Perils and Pleasures in the Sexual Metropolis, 1918–1957* (Chicago: University of Chicago Press, 2005); A. McLaren, *Twentieth-Century Sexuality: A History* (Oxford: Blackwell, 1999); F. Mort, *Dangerous Sexualities: Medico-Moral Politics in England since 1830*, 2nd edition (London: Routledge, 2000); R. Nye, ed., *Sexuality* (Oxford: Oxford University Press, 1999); A. L. Stoler, *Race and the Education of Desire: Foucault's "History of Sexuality" and the Colonial Order of Things* (Durham, NC: Duke University Press, 1995).

Chapter 3   Gender and Other Relations of Difference

On philanthropy, see D. Elliott, *The Angel Out of the House: Philanthropy and Gender in Nineteenth-Century England* (Charlottesville: University of Virginia Press, 2002); V. Nguyen-Marshall, *In Search of Moral Authority: The Discourse on Poverty, Poor Relief and Charity in French Colo-*

nial Vietnam (Oxford: Peter Lang, 2009). On slavery and post-emancipation society, see S. D. Amussen, *Caribbean Exchanges: Slavery and the Transformation of English Society, 1640–1700* (Chapel Hill: University of North Carolina Press, 2007); G. Heuman and J. Walvin, *The Slavery Reader* (London: Routledge, 2003); M. Nishida, *Slavery and Identity: Ethnicity, Gender and Race in Salvador, Brazil 1808–1888* (Bloomington: Indiana University Press, 2003); D. Paton, *No Bond but the Law: Punishment, Race, and Gender in Jamaican State Formation 1780–1870* (Durham, NC: Duke University Press, 2004); H. Rosen, *Terror in the Heart of Freedom: Citizenship, Sexual Violence, and the Meaning of Race in the Post-Emancipation South* (Chapel Hill: University of North Carolina Press, 2009); P. Scully and D. Paton, *Gender and Slave Emancipation in the Atlantic World* (Durham, NC: Duke University Press, 2005). On empire and colonialism, see A. Burton, ed., *Gender, Sexuality and Colonial Modernities* (London: Routledge, 1999); C. Crais and P. Scully, *Sarah Baartman and the Hottentot Venus: A Ghost Story and a Biography* (Princeton: Princeton University Press, 2008); C. Hall, ed., *Cultures of Empire: Colonizers in Britain and the Empire in the Nineteenth and Twentieth Centuries. A Reader* (New York: Routledge, 2000); P. Levine, ed., *Gender and Empire* (Oxford: Oxford University Press, 2004); P. Levine, *Prostitution, Race and Politics: Policing Venereal Disease in the British Empire* (London: Routledge, 2003); A. McClintock, *Imperial Leather: Race, Gender and Sexuality in the Colonial Movement* (New York: Routledge, 1995); R. Pierson and N. Chaudhuri, eds, *Nation, Empire, Colony: Historicizing Gender and Race* (Bloomington: Indiana University Press, 1998); J. Clancy-Smith and F. Gouda, eds, *Domesticating the Empire: Race, Gender, and Family Life in French and Dutch Colonialism* (Charlottesville: University of Virginia Press, 1998); A. L. Stoler, *Carnal Knowledge and Imperial Power: Race and the Intimate in Colonial Rule* (Berkeley: University of California Press, 2002); K. Wilson, *The Island Race: Englishness, Empire and Gender in the Eighteenth Century* (London: Routledge, 2003); A. Woollacott, *Gender and Empire* (Basingstoke: Palgrave Macmillan, 2006).

Chapter 4   Men and Masculinity

On the issue of men and violence, see L. Braudy, *From Chivalry to Terrorism: War and the Changing Nature of Masculinity* (New York: Alfred A. Knopf, 2003); S. Stern, *The Secret History of Gender: Women, Men, and Power in Late Colonial Mexico* (Chapel Hill: University of North Carolina Press, 1995). For overviews and essays on men and masculinity in various societies and time periods, see B. Clements, R. Friedman, and D. Healey, eds, *Russian Masculinities in History and Culture* (Basingstoke: Palgrave, 2002); R. Connell, *Masculinities*, 2nd edition (Cambridge: Polity, 2005); C. E. Forth, *Masculinity in the Modern West: Gender, Civilization and the Body* (Basingstoke: Palgrave Macmillan, 2008); T. Hitchcock and M. Cohen, *English Masculinities 1660–1800* (London: Longman, 1999); M. Kessel, "The 'Whole Man': The Longing for a Masculine World in Nineteenth-Century Germany," *Gender & History* 15 (2003): 1–31; M. Kimmel, *Manhood in America: A Cultural History*, 2nd edition (Oxford: Oxford University Press, 2006); L. Lindsay and S. Miescher, eds, *Men and Masculinities in Modern Africa* (Westport, CT: Heinemann, 2003); K. Louie, *Theorizing Chinese Masculinity: Society and Gender in China* (Cambridge: Cambridge University Press, 2002); J. Martinez and C. Lowrie, "Colonial Constructions of Masculinity: Transforming Aboriginal Australian Men into 'Houseboys,'" *Gender & History* 21 (2009): 305–23; J. Tosh, *Manliness and Masculinity in Nineteenth-Century Britain: Essays on Gender, Family and Empire* (Harlow: Pearson Longman, 2005). For a critique of histories of masculinity, see T. Ditz, "The New Men's History and the Peculiar Absence of Gendered Power: Some Remedies from Early American Gender History," *Gender & History* 16 (2004): 1–35.

Chapter 5   Gender and Historical Knowledge

On Indians and colonial encounters, see J. Barr, *Peace Came in the Form of a Woman: Indians and Spaniards in the Texas*

Borderlands (Chapel Hill: University of North Carolina Press, 2007); T. Perdue, *Cherokee Women: Gender and Culture Change, 1700–1835* (Omaha: University of Nebraska Press, 1998); C. Saunt, *Black, White, and Indian: Race and the Unmaking of an American Family* (Oxford: Oxford University Press, 2005). For overviews and essay collections on revolution, politics, and war, see A. Timm and J. Sanborn, *Gender, Sex and the Shaping of Modern Europe: A History from the French Revolution to the Present Day* (New York: Berg, 2007); S. Dudink, K. Hagemann, and J. Tosh, eds, *Masculinities in Politics and War: Gendering Modern History* (Manchester: Manchester University Press, 2004). On the various revolutions, see L. Dubois, *Avengers of the New World* (Cambridge, MA: Harvard University Press, 2004) on the Haitian revolution; D. Davidson, *France after Revolution: Urban Life, Gender and the New Social Order* (Cambridge, MA: Harvard University Press, 2007); J. Heuer, *The Family and the Nation: Gender and Citizenship in Revolutionary France, 1789–1830* (Ithaca: Cornell University Press, 2005); K. Davies, *Catherine Macauley and Mercy Otis Warren: The Revolutionary Atlantic and the Politics of Gender* (Oxford: Oxford University Press, 2005); S. Smith, *Gender and the Mexican Revolution: Yucatan Women and the Realities of Patriarchy* (Chapel Hill: University of North Carolina Press, 2009). On war, see S. Grayzel, *Women's Identities at War: Gender, Motherhood, and Politics in Britain and France during the First World War* (Chapel Hill: University of North Carolina Press, 1999); P. Krebs, *Gender, Race, and Writing of Empire: Public Discourse and the Boer War* (Cambridge: Cambridge University Press, 1999); J. Meyer, *Men of War: Masculinity and the First World War in Britain* (Basingstoke: Palgrave Macmillan, 2009); R. Smith, *Jamaican Volunteers in the First World War: Race, Masculinity and the Development of National Consciousness* (Manchester: Manchester University Press, 2004); P. Summerfield and C. Peniston-Bird, *Contesting Home Defence: Men, Women and the Home Guard in the Second World War* (Manchester: Manchester University Press, 2007). On gender and post-war reconstruction, see C. Duchen and I. Bandhauer-Schoffmann, eds, *When the War Was Over: Women, War and Peace in Europe, 1940–1956* (London: Leicester University Press,

2000); D. Herzog, *Sex after Fascism: Memory and Morality in Twentieth-Century Germany* (Princeton: Princeton University Press, 2005); M. L. Roberts, *Civilization without Sexes: Reconstructing Gender in Postwar France* (Chicago: University of Chicago Press, 1994); also see the forum on "The 'Remasculinization' of Germany in the 1950s" with essays by R. Moeller, H. Fehrenbach, and S. Jeffords, *Signs* 24 (1998): 101–69. On nation and citizenship, see I. Blom, K. Hagemann, and C. Hall, eds, *Gendered Nations: Nationalisms and Gender Order in the Long Nineteenth Century* (Oxford: Berg, 2000); K. Canning and S. Rose, *Gender, Citizenships and Subjectivities* (Oxford: Blackwell, 2002); S. Dudink, K. Hagemann, and A. Clark, eds, *Representing Masculinity: Male Citizenship in Modern Western Culture* (Basingstoke: Palgrave, 2007); C. Hall, K. McClelland, and J. Rendall, *Defining the Victorian Nation: Class, Race, Gender and the British Reform Act of 1867* (Cambridge: Cambridge University Press, 2000); S. Heathorn, *For Home, Country and Race: Constructing Gender, Class, and Englishness in the Elementary School 1880–1914* (Toronto: University of Toronto Press, 1999); J. Hogan, ed., *Gender, Race and National Identity: Nations of Flesh and Blood* (New York: Routledge, 2009); L. Kerber, *No Constitutional Right to be Ladies: Women and the Obligations of Citizenship* (New York: Hill & Wang, 1998); J. Surkis, *Sexing the Citizen: Morality and Masculinity in France 1870–1920* (Ithaca: Cornell University Press, 2006). For overviews and essays on labor and industrialization, see A. Baron, "Masculinity, the Embodied Male Worker, and the Historian's Gaze," *International Labor and Working-Class History* 69 (2006): 143–60; L. Frader and S. Rose, eds, *Gender and Class in Modern Europe* (Ithaca: Cornell University Press, 1996); L. Frader, "Labor History after the Gender Turn: Transatlantic Cross-Currents and Research Agendas," *International Labor and Working-Class History* 63 (2003): 21–31; K. Honeyman, *Women, Gender and Industrialization in England, 1700–1870* (Basingstoke: Macmillan, 2000); Eileen Yeo, "Gender in Labour and Working-Class History," in M. van der Linden and L. van Voss, eds, *Class and Other Identities: Gender, Religion and Ethnicity in the Writing of European Labour History* (New York: Berghahn Books, 2002): 73–87. For studies of gender and labor in various societies, see K. Canning, *Languages of Labor and Gender: Female Factory Work in Germany, 1850–1914* (Ithaca: Cornell University Press, 1996); L. Downs, *Manufacturing Inequality: Gender Division in the French and British Metalworking Industries, 1914–39* (Ithaca: Cornell University Press, 1995); W. Z. Goldman, *Women at the Gates: Gender and Industry in Stalin's Russia* (Cambridge: Cambridge University Press, 2002).

Chapter 6   Assessing "Turns" and New Directions

For assessments of various cultural approaches to history, see E. Clark, *History, Theory, Text: History and the Linguistic Turn* (Cambridge, MA: Harvard University Press, 2004); G. Eley, *A Crooked Line: From Cultural History to the History of Society* (Ann Arbor: University of Michigan Press, 2005); G. Lerner, "US Women's History: Past, Present and Future," *Journal of Women's History* 16 (2004): 10–27; G. Spiegel, "Introduction," in G. Spiegel, ed., *Practicing History: New Directions in Historical Writing after the Linguistic Turn* (New York: Routledge, 2005): 1–31. On world/global/ transnational history, see L. Edwards and M. Roces, *Women's Suffrage in Asia: Gender, Nationalism and Democracy* (London: Routledge/Curzon, 2004); L. Rupp, "Teaching about Transnational Feminisms," *Radical History Review* 20 (2008): 191–7; P. Sharpe, ed., *Women, Gender and Labour Migration: Historical and Global Perspectives* (London: Routledge, 2001); B. Smith, ed., *Women's History in Global Perspective*, 4 volumes (Urbana: University of Illinois Press, 2004); B. Smith, ed., *Oxford Encyclopedia of Women in World History*, 4 volumes (Oxford: Oxford University Press, 2008); A. Walthall, ed., *Servants of the Dynasty: Palace Women in World History* (Berkeley: University of California Press, 2008); M. Wiesner-Hanks, "World History and the History of Women, Gender, and Sexuality," *Journal of World History* 18 (2007): 53–67; J. Zinsser, "Women's History, World History, and the Construction of New Narratives,"

Journal of Women's History 12 (2000): 196–206. On subjectivity and psychoanalytical approaches, see R. Braidotti, "Identity, Subjectivity and Difference: A Critical Genealogy," in G. Griffen and R. Braidotti, eds, *Thinking Differently: A Reader in European Women's Studies* (London: Zed Books, 2002): 158–80; N. Mansfield, *Subjectivity: Theories of the Self from Freud to Haraway* (New York: New York University Press, 2000); M. Roper, *The Secret Battle: Emotional Survival in the Great War* (Manchester: Manchester University Press, 2009); P. Summerfield, *Reconstructing Women's Wartime Lives: Discourse and Subjectivity in Oral Histories of the Second World War* (Manchester: Manchester University Press, 1998). Also see the essays in "Feature: Psychoanalysis and History," *History Workshop Journal* 45 (1998): 135–221.

Index

abolitionism 6, 40–2
Adams, Abigail 82
Alexander, Sally 8
American Civil War 6, 10, 69
American Revolution
  British colonies 81, 90
  French involvement 84
  gender differences 83
  post-war era 118
  religion 83–4
  republicanism 95
  women's role 82
American War of
    Independence: see
    American Revolution
Anderson, Benedict 89–90
Anglo-Indian community 51,
  70–1
anti-imperialists 70
anti-Semitism 65–6
Ashplant, Timothy 108–9
Asia, Central 22–3
Asia, Southeast 33
Australia 73, 116

Bacon, Nathaniel 62
Bacon's Rebellion 61–2, 78

Ballantyne, Tony 117
Baptist Church 84
Baptist missionaries 41
Barbados 42–3, 48
Beard, Mary 4
Beckles, Hilary McD. 47–8
Bederman, Gail 66–7, 68, 69,
  72–3
Berkeley, William 60, 61
biological differences 34
Bloch, Ruth 83
Bock, Gisela 37
body
  female 19, 21, 105–6, 110
  history 20–1
  male 19, 21, 64–5
  politics 21, 22
  religion 21–2
  sexuality 23–4
  subjectivities 107
Bourke, Joanna 21
boyhood 63
Bridenthal, Renate 5, 12
Britain
  abolitionism 40–1
  American colonies 80–3
  American Revolution 81, 90

Britain (cont.)
  boxing 73–4
  feminist history 7–8, 9
  industrialization 111
  public/private spheres 8–9
  universal male suffrage 97–8
  working-class women 8
  World War I 97
British Columbia 51–2
British Empire
  Caribbean 44
  gender/sexuality 50–1
  India 53, 114–15
  prostitution 51
  venereal disease 33
brothels 31, 33–4
  see also prostitution
Brown, Kathleen 45–7, 61–4,
    107, 112
Burke, Peter 106
Burns, Tommy 73
Burton, Antoinette 42, 43,
    117
Butler, Eleanor 29
Butler, Josephine 32
Butler, Judith 20
Bynum, Carolyn Walker 21–2

Canada 51–2, 118
Canning, Kathleen 21, 103,
    105–6, 107
Cape Colony 49–50
capitalism 8
Caribbean 41, 44, 80, 82
  see also Barbados
Carolina 48, 49
Catholic Church 26, 27, 81
Chamberlain, Mary 119–20
Chartism 99
Chauncey, George 28
China
  family 93–5
  gender concept 15–16
  industrialization 111
  patriarchy 94

women's suffrage 94
  women's traditional roles 94
Christianity
  asceticism 21–2
  muscular 76–7
  see also specific sects
citizenship
  active/passive 85
  gender differences 82, 89,
    90–1, 115
  honor 91
  military service 95–6
  political 80, 83, 101
  property requirements 99
  service 97
civil society 22
Clark, Alice 4
Clark, Anna 98–100
class
  domesticity 40
  home visiting 39
  masculinity 109
  philanthropic
    organizations 43
  physical state 66
  plantations 61–2
  race/gender 10, 36–7, 38–9,
    43, 44, 50, 51–2
  volunteer work 38–9
  welfare reforms 39, 40
  see also middle class;
    working class
colonial rule 142–3
  America, North 80–3
  France 54, 82
  gender/class 44
  gender/sexuality 54–5, 80
  interracial sexual
    relations 50, 53
  marriage 46
  masculinity 70–1, 78
  power 70–1
  prostitution 33
  racial hierarchy 13
Communist Party of China 95

comparative analysis, global history 111
concubinage 51
Congregational Church 83–4
Connell, Raewyn 20–1, 24, 58
Contagious Diseases Acts 32, 42
Cook, James 117
Cott, Nancy 7, 14
Cuba 38–9, 69, 70, 116
cultural turn 13, 145–6

Davidoff, Leonore 9, 15, 74
Davis, Madeline D. 30
Davis, Natalie Zemon 11
de Gouges, Olympe 85, 87
deconstructionism 104
Derrida, Jacques 104
Desan, Suzanne 88–9
difference, relations of 140–1
  biological 34
  bodily 18–19, 20, 34
  cultural 15, 81
  natural 3, 19
  sexual 18–19, 103
  women's history 36
  see also gender differences
discourse concept 13
divorce laws 88–9
domesticity 40, 75, 76, 100
  see also public/private spheres
Dreyfus Affair 65–6
Dublin, Thomas 9–10
DuBois, Ellen Carol 36–7
Dudink, Stefan 58
Dutch East Indies 51, 53
Dutch Republic 89

economic transformations 68–9
effeminacy 57, 58, 70–1, 78
Egypt 92–3
Eley, Geoff 103
emigration 119

Enlightenment 19–20, 82
evangelicalism 83–4

fairies, as term for homosexual men 28
family
  China 93–5
  Egypt 92–3
  French Republic 90–1
  men 57–8, 74–5
  as metaphors 90, 91
  missionaries 41
family economy 8, 119
fatherhood 74
Faust, Drew Gilpin 14
femininity 3, 43, 81
feminism
  black/Latina 36
  capitalism 8
  human rights 5
  imperialism 42
  India 42, 115
  and Marxism 95
  radical 10
  second-wave 5
  socialism 8, 11
feminist historians 103–4, 112–13, 115
feminist history 7–8, 9, 11, 80, 103
Fischer, Kirsten 48–9, 112
Forth, Christopher E. 65–6
Foucault, Michel 25, 104
Frader, Laura 113
France
  African workers 53–4
  citizen-soldiers 95–6
  colonial rule 54, 82
  Constitution 85
  duels 64
  and English 81
  gender concept 15
  Islam 22, 23
  manhood 65–6
  Napoleonic Era 95, 96

France (cont.)
  women workers 54
  women's history 6, 82,
    85–6
  World War I 53–4
  see also French Republic;
    French Revolution
Francis, Martin 76–7
Franco-Prussian War 65
fraternity 86, 90, 98–9
French Republic
  established 85
  family 90–1
  manhood 86
  motherhood 88
  visual female
    representations 87–8
French Revolution
  body/politics 22
  clothing 35
  patriarchy 88–9
  women 82, 84–7, 88–9

Gabaccia, Donna 119
gay rights 25
gay subculture 28
  see also homosexuality
gender
  beauty 23–4
  bodily differences 18–19
  as category 11–12, 16, 17
  cultural differences 15
  defined 2–3
  femininity 43
  historical knowledge 142–5
  ideologies 68
  imperialism 42, 114
  labor 113
  migration 118–19
  misrecognition 117
  morality 40–1
  performativity 20
  politics 100
  power 4, 13, 14, 58, 81
  public/private spheres 38

race/class 10, 36–7, 38–9,
    43, 44, 50, 51–2
  Scott 13, 17
  sex 3, 17–18, 34, 139–40
  sexuality 14, 50–1, 54–5,
    65, 80
  slavery 80, 112
  suffrage movement 69–70
  women's culture 11
Gender & History journal 15
gender differences
  American Revolution 83
  biological 18
  citizenship 82, 89, 90–1,
    115
  clothing 22, 34–5
  cultural construction of
    116–17, 121
  migration 120
  politics 83
  post-emancipation
    society 44–5
  scientific knowledge 18
  social constructions 2–3,
    13–14
  wages 111
George III 82
Germany
  civil society 22
  clothing 35
  labor politics 105–6
  militarism 71
  prostitution 33–4
  sexuality 30–1
  textile industry 21
  witchcraft 110
  women workers 21, 105–6
  women's history 6
Gilmore, David 58
Girondins 86–7
global history 110–11
Glosser, Susan 94
Gordon, Charles W. 76–7
Gordon, Linda 38
Greece, ancient 22, 26

Greenberg, Amy 68–9
Grosz, Elizabeth 21
Gullace, Nicoletta 97

Hagemann, Karen 96
Hall, Catherine 41–2, 44, 74
Halperin, David 26
headscarf controversy 23
heterosexuality 27, 28, 64–5
Hewitt, Nancy 38–9
Hindus 71, 114
history 1–2, 102
  biographical approach 108
  body 20–1
  cultural approaches 145–6
  psychoanalytic approach
    108
  revisionism 103
  women's activism 4–5
Hoerder, Dirk 118
Hoff, Joan 13
Hoganson, Kristin L. 69–70,
  78
homosexuality 25–6, 66
  inverts 28
  see also same-sex
    relationships
Hughes, Michael J. 96
Hull, Isabel 22, 30–1
Hunt, Lynn 22, 85–7, 88

identity
  formation 109–10
  lesbian 30
  psychic/social 108–9
  sexual 27
illegitimate children 88–9
immigrants 39, 51–2, 119–20
  Caribbean 119–20
  Chinese 40
  see also migration
imperialism 42, 53, 68,
  114–15
  see also British Empire
indentured servants 46, 47

India
  British imperialism 53,
    114–15
  feminism 42, 115
  masculinities 70–1
  nationalist movement 71, 72
  prostitution 51, 72
Indian Rebellion 71–2
Indians, Native American 81
Indochina 53
industrialization 111
Iran 23–4, 91
Ireland 71, 72
Islam 22, 23

Jacobins 86–7, 88
Jamaica 41
Japan 26, 93
Jeffries, Jim 73
Johnson, Jack 73
Jones, Jacqueline 9, 10, 44, 45
Juster, Susan 83–4

Karras, Ruth Mazo 31, 59
Kelly-Gadol, Joan 11
Kemal, Mustafa (Atatürk) 93
Kennedy, Elizabeth
  Lapovsky 30
Kerber, Linda 6
Kessler-Harris, Alice 9–10,
  113
Kimmel, Michael S. 56, 68
kinship networks 52, 90, 117
knights 59
Koonz, Claudia 5, 12

labor
  gender 113
  politics of 105–6
  as property 99
  reproductive 48
  sexual division of 10, 44,
    113
  unionism 9
  world history 113

Ladies National Association 32
Ladies of Llangollen 29
Lake, Marilyn 115–16
Landes, Joan 91
Laqueur, Thomas 19–20
Latin America 53
lesbianism 25, 28, 30, 35
Levine, Philippa 33, 50–1
Liddington, Jill 8
linguistic turn 13, 102, 145–6
Little, Ann 80–1
Lombard, Anne 62–3, 82
London 27, 39, 105
London Feminist History
    Group 10
Louis XVI 85
Lutherans 31–2

McClelland, Keith 100
McCormack, Matthew 97–8
McDevitt, Patrick 73–4
McDonnell, Michael,
    A. 117–18
McLaren, Angus 66
male bonding 31–2, 59
manhood
    American 67–8
    Anglo-American 64
    behavior 58
    cultural codes 77–8
    duels 64
    elites/male honor 61–2
    entitlement 98
    France 65–6
    French Republic 86
    honor 61–2, 64–5, 91
    independence, economic 60,
        61, 63, 67, 82, 98
    martial 68–9
    middle-class 66–7
    New England 82
    politics 89
    property requirements 99
    restrained 68–9
    as status 60, 78

tests of 58–9
violence 61
see also masculinity; men
Manifest Destiny concept 68–9
Marie Antoinette 85, 86
marriage
    à la façon du pays 52
    colonialism 46
    companionate 75
    interracial 49, 51–2
    men 74
    missionaries 41
    slaves 47–8
Marshall, David B. 76, 77
martial races 71–3
    Gurkhas, Nepalese 71, 72
    Scottish Highlanders 71, 72
Marx, Karl 7, 8, 11
Marxist influences 7–8, 11, 95
masculinity 142
    adventure 76
    class 109
    colonial 70–1, 78
    crisis of 65–6, 78
    as cultural construct 78–9
    domesticity 75
    hegemonic 58, 61
    heroic 22
    heterosexual 96
    initiation rituals 59
    martial qualities 68–9, 96
    military 71–2
    norms 57
    post-war 21
    power 70–1
    race 73–4
    sexuality 35
    World War I 76, 109
    see also manhood; men
Massachusetts Bay
    Colony 62–3
masturbation 30–1
maternity: *see* motherhood
May Fourth Movement 93, 95
Mayo, Katherine 114

men
  Bengali 13, 70–1, 78
  emigration 119
  English 13, 59–60, 70–1, 78, 81
  Euro-Canadian 52–3
  family 74–5
  fatherhood 74
  as gendered historical subjects 56
  institutional settings 57–8
  Jewish 65–6
  marriage 57–8, 74
  medieval 59–60
  middle-class 75
  politically privileged 20
  subjectivities 77
  working-class 66, 100
  see also manhood;
    masculinity; patriarchy
Mexico 69
middle class
  family men 75
  manhood 66–7
  New England 62–3
  US women's history 36
Midgley, Clare 40–1
migration 118–19, 120
Mink, Gwendolyn 39
miscegenation 53
missionaries 40, 41
Modern Girl 115
Morgan, Jennifer 48
motherhood
  body 110
  domesticity 75
  French Republic 88
  Germany 21, 39, 75
  men/masculinity 108
  US 39
  witch trials 110
  women workers 106

Najmabadi, Afsaneh 23–4, 91
Napoleonic Code 89

Napoleonic Era 95, 96
Nationalist Party, China 94
nationality 71–2
nationhood 80, 82, 89–90, 101
Native American Indians 81
nature 19
Nazism 33–4
Netherlands 26, 27
neurasthenia 66
new cultural history concept 106–7
New Culture Movement 93, 94
New England 62–3, 81, 82
  see also specific colonies
New Women 4, 70
New York 9, 28
Newton, Judith 11–12
Newton, Melanie 42–3
Nicaragua 69
Nield, Keith 103
Norris, Jill 8
Northrop, Douglas 22–3
Norton, Mary Beth 82
Nye, Robert 64–5

oral histories 30, 119–20
Oren, Laura 8
othering 37, 38, 43, 56, 140–1
Ottoman Empire 92, 93
Outram, Dorinda 22

Pacific Islanders 117
Paine, Thomas 82
Paris 84–5
patriarchy
  China 94
  French Revolution 88–9
  power 7–8, 14
  racialized 46–7
  slavery 45–7
  Venezuela 91
  violence 62, 63–4

patriarchy (cont.)
  Virginia 61–4
  and womanhood 6
People's Republic of China 94
Perry, Adele 51–2
philanthropic organizations
    43
Philippine–American war 70,
    78, 116
Pinchbeck, Ivy 4
politics
  body 21, 22
  citizenship 80, 83, 101
  gender 100
  gender differences 83
  manhood 89
  privilege 20
  radical 99
  women's participation 22
Polynesian society 117
Pomeranz, Kenneth 111–12
Ponsonby, Sarah 29
post-emancipation society 44–5
post-modernism 102–3
post-structuralism 12–13,
    14–15, 16, 102–3, 104–5
power
  colonial rule 70–1
  gender 4, 13, 14, 58, 81
  masculinity 70–1
  patriarchy 7–8, 14
Power, Eileen 4
Procida, Mary 51
property relations 7–8, 63,
    88–9
prostitution
  British Empire 51
  colonial rule 33
  history of 31
  India 51, 72
  London 105
  male bonding 31–2
  public health 34
  regulation of 33
  and sodomites 27–8

Protestant Reformation 26–7
public/private spheres 6, 8–9,
    38
Puff, Helmut 26
Puritanism 62–4

Qing dynasty 94
queer, as term for male
    homosexuals 28

race
  abolitionism 41–2
  boxing 73–4
  class/gender 10, 36–7, 38–9,
    43, 44, 50, 51–2
  hierarchy 13, 41
  masculinity 73–4
  Modern Girl 115
  punishment 49
  rape cases 49–50
  sexual relations,
    interracial 48–9, 50, 53
  sexuality 29–30, 35, 49
  welfare reforms 38, 40
RAF pilots 76
rape cases 49–50
Reform Acts 98, 99, 100
religion 21–3, 26, 83–4
Representation of the People
    Act 97, 100
republicanism 95
Roberts, Frederick 72
Roosevelt, Theodore 67–8
Roper, Lyndal 31–2, 109–10
Roper, Michael 77, 107–8,
    109
Ross, Ellen 39
Rowbotham, Sheila 7–8
Ruiz, Vicki 36–7
Russia 71
Ryan, Mary 11–12, 17, 83

San Francisco 39–40
Sawtelle, May 40
Schiebinger, Londa 18, 19

scientific knowledge 18, 19–20, 64–5, 104
Scott, Joan
  gender history 12
  linguistic approach 107
  post-structuralism 14–15, 104–5
  sex/gender 13, 17
  veiling 23
Scully, Pamela 49–50
Segal, Lynne 68
sex 3, 17–18, 27, 34, 139–40
sex tourism 118
sexuality
  body 23–4
  feared 32
  friendships 7
  gender 14, 50–1, 54–5, 65, 80
  Germany 30–1
  Greece, ancient 26
  history of 24–5
  masculinity 35
  men 51
  military strength 34
  race 29–30, 35, 49
  repression 28
  same-sex relationships 25–6, 27, 28–30, 35
  scientific knowledge 104
  violence 49
Shah, Nyan 39–40
Shepard, Alexandra 60–1, 62
Sikhs, Punjabi 71, 72
Sinha, Mrinalini 13, 70–1, 78, 91, 114
slavery
  African women 47–8
  castration as punishment 49
  emancipation 41–2
  gender 80, 112
  hereditary 46
  marriage 47–8
  patriarchy 45–7
  plantations 47–8, 61–2

  punishment 49
  sexual division of labor 10
  Virginia 45–7, 62
Smith-Rosenberg, Carroll 7
Society of Revolutionary Republican Women 85
sodomites 26–8
soldiers
  letters 77, 107–8
  nationality 71–2
  women as 96
South Africa 49–50, 73, 116
Southampton 31
Soviet Union 23
Spanish–American war 70, 78
Spruill, Julia 4
Stansell, Christine 10
Stead, W. T. 105
Stearns, Peter 113–14
Stoics 22
Stoler, Ann 51
Stovall, Tyler 53, 54
Streets, Heather 71–2
Stuard, Susan 12
students 59, 60
subjectivities
  body 107
  culture 110
  gendered 79, 110, 120–1
  history of 109
  men 77
  sexual 28–9
  World War I 108
suffrage movement
  universal male 97–8, 99
  women's suffrage movement 8, 42, 68, 69–70
Sun Yatsen 94

Tahiti 117
Tampa, Florida 38–9
text, as concept 13
textile industry 9–10, 21
theory wars 103–4, 107

Timm, Annette 33–4
Tosh, John 58, 74–5
translocal relations 117
trans-national approach 112, 114, 115–16, 119–20
True Womanhood, Cult of 6
Trumbach, Randolph 26, 27, 28, 31
Turkey 93

United States of America
  diplomacy 78
  economic transformations 68–9
  expansionism 69
  feminist history 9–10
  foreign policy 70
  gender/women's culture 11
  Manifest Destiny concept 68–9
  neurasthenia 66
  welfare reforms 39
  women's history 6, 36
Uzbekistan 23

Van Kirk, Sylvia 52
veiling 22–3
venereal disease 21, 33
Venezuela 91
Versailles Treaty 93
Vicinus, Martha 29, 30
violence 49, 61, 62, 63–4, 105, 142
Virginia 45–7, 61–4, 62, 78
volunteer work 38–9

wages/gender differences 111
Walkowitz, Judith 11–12, 32, 105, 106
warfare 21, 80, 96–7, 101
Warren, Mercy Otis 82
Weeks, Jeffrey 25
welfare policies 38–40
Welter, Barbara 6

West Indies 42, 43, 44, 47–8
White, Deborah Gray 44, 45
Wilson, Kathleen 117
witch trials 110
Wollstonecraft, Mary 87, 99
womanhood 6, 14, 38, 49–50, 70
women
  aboriginal 52–3
  activism 4–5, 85–6
  African 47–8
  American Revolution 82
  black 9, 10, 44–5
  citizenship 82
  dependence 82
  emigration 119
  fraternity 86, 90
  French Revolution 84–5, 88–9
  Latina 36, 38–9
  as other 56
  private sphere 6–7
  records of lives 3–4
  slavery 47–8
  as soldiers 96
  Turkey 93
  white 46–7
  working-class 8, 9, 10, 30, 44–5
  see also femininity; feminism; maternity; womanhood; women workers
women workers
  female bodies 105–6
  France 54
  Germany 21, 105–6
  as mothers 106
  textile industry 9–10, 21
  unionism 9
women's culture 7, 11
women's history
  differences 36
  as discipline 5–6
  French 6, 82, 85–6
  radical feminism 10

US 36, 82–3
white, middle-class 36
women's movement 67
women's rights 5, 89, 99
women's suffrage 85, 94
working class 8, 9, 10, 30,
    44–5, 66, 100
world history
      approach 110–11, 113

World War I
  British women 97
  France 53–4
  letters 77, 107–8
  masculinity 76, 109
  men's bodies 21
  subjectivities 108
  Turkey 93
World War II 76